Praise for *The Bones & Brea
Masculine, and the Wild Soul*

"Inside each one of us swirls and surges a mysterious longing, which L.R. Heartsong knows to be the essential catalyst for the larger, unique and more dangerous life that awaits each one of us. *The Bones and Breath* offers a persuasive revisioning of masculinity, one that supports both men and women in our search for a meaningful and passionate way to participate in our great transformative times." ~ Bill Plotkin, author of *Soulcraft: Crossing into the Mysteries of Nature and Psyche*, and *Wild Mind: A Field Guide to the Human Psyche*

"This book is a must read for every person looking to live an inspired, conscious and soulful life. I read this book in three days and couldn't wait to pick it back up each time I put it down. I am considering starting at the beginning for a second read! I have been walking through my days inspired to embody every moment. I have not found a book that inspires me as much as this one has in a long, long time. Thank you to the author for his great insight, poetic prose and authentic soulfulness. Can't wait for the second book!" ~ RS, Amazon review

"What I know is that my journey [with the book] is not only healing myself, but also the generations who have come before me and those who will come after. Thank you for helping me as a husband, son, friend, uncle, and role model."
~ Nick V.

"Every once in a while a book comes along that blows your socks off. And this is one that has just come into my life... a book about the Sacred Masculine that goes so deep and is written so beautifully, I'm truly in awe. I challenge all of my male friends who want to embrace their masculinity and sacredness in these interesting times of great change and burgeoning of the Divine Feminine to read this book. I challenge all men who seek to be conscious and in touch with their soul to find a copy and absorb it. Be guided and inspired by it, and more. How many of you will take this challenge? This book will take you deeper. This is a truly powerful work. And quite beneficial for us women too. Quite. LR Heartsong's writing is so eloquent, it veritably dances off the page. If there is such thing as writer's envy, I suspect I have it towards him but that's okay. It is such a joy to read writing that takes your breath away. Deep joy." ~ Mare Cromwell, author of *The Great Mother Bible*

"I'm forever grateful this book found its way to me, and I look forward to my copy becoming even more lovingly well worn with each time I return to its treasures. Every chapter is humming with resonance, synchronicity and poetry." ~ Paul P.

"It is beautifully written, and there is considerable wisdom on each page." ~ Thomas B.

"I love it. Serious, dense, light and elegant... you have the writer's touch." ~ Carolyn Brigit Flynn, author of *Communion: In Praise of the Sacred Earth*

"Reading your words is, for me, like coming to the spring and finding the mossy cup where the god left it..." ~ Dixie G.

"Thank you from the bottom of my heart for writing it. I cannot tell you how your book speaks to the very fiber of my being... how it has, this week, inspired a new depth of understanding of what I am doing." ~ Richard S.

"The prose is lush, a language embodiment of Eros..." ~ Hari H.

"... Heartsong has elegantly opened doors of insight and invitation to both men and women here. I wondered if the fact that I am a woman would deter me from this book, but it absolutely did not; rather it offered me a deliciousness for both my own inner masculine and feminine. I am deeply grateful for the page after page of beauty, remembering, and possibility that I found here." ~ Jade S.

"With every breath as I read every word and every page, I was brought right home – straight to my self, my core, my being. My truth had been in my bones all along. Thank you for having led the way!" ~ Ioannis

"Sensitive, soulful and insightful, a refreshingly unique, beautifully written, transformative book, as relevant to women as to men." ~ SJR, Amazon UK review

"I read the first chapter on the plane, then had to stop as I needed to do the Soul Skills 'Wandering Walk' exercise. This book resonates with me like nothing I have ever read. It feels like a guidebook to finding the 'me' that is yearning to come out." ~ Nathan D.

"Love, love, loving your writing, you transcend me. Your words are a gift to the world. Thank you for writing!" ~ Dawn Breslin, TV & Radio presenter, best-selling Hay House author, Emotional Wellbeing Coach (UK)

Reader comments from the *Soul Artist Journal*

"I've been reading your archives. Weeks ago, I'd meant to begin reading – one or two every now and then, I'd thought, but rather I've found myself reading and re-reading everything I could find. You are an amazing creature. Of all the things we've piled up for 'someday', perhaps first on my own list is to speak to you at length about your writing and to encourage you to publish further. More widely. *Bravissimo,* you are... " ~ Marlena de Blasi, internationally bestselling author of *A Thousand Days in Venice* and *A Thousand Days in Tuscany*

"Your writing – words chosen, scenes described, emotions created – touches me like nothing else. It is a beautiful gift that leaves me vacant and overflowing at the same time. Thank you is not enough for what you give." ~ Cindy H.

"You have this gift of being able to fearlessly write absolute raw emotion. It is beautiful." ~ Susan Marie

"Every time I read your posts, I am taken. In. All the way. The trembling depth of your honesty and vulnerability. The courage to keep moving bare against earth, sky, along the page of your journey. The sacred masculinity is so poignant and needed in this world with the over load and over indulgence of the sacred feminine, I can only imagine someone will recognize that your work needs to be gifted to the world. Thank you for your tremendous perseverance, commitment and heart. You are a gem among men." ~ Leslie C.

"A reminder... that's what you are... a beautiful reminder. It's time to put down my 'stones' and dip my feet into the ocean. What a gift you've given yet again. Thank you!" ~ Gabrielle R.

"Always beautifully said. Thank you for sharing your lovely musings with us during the last four years! I look forward each and every week to your posting, as it *always* finds words that speak to me. I found you during your podcast time (I miss that BTW) and still play them when I need a bit of a 'return to nature' reminder. You are truly appreciated and I am ever grateful for your sharing!" ~ Susan H.

"Once again, you lift my soul to a higher place. Thank you and blessings!"
~ Shauna Z.

"Thank you for your beautiful words." ~ Barry S.

"I cried as I read this for it matches my world perfectly, and because tonight I feel the world's woes, and her pains as well as ours. Thank you for voicing it for me too. I'm an artist and see and draw, paint or create how I'm feeling but sometimes words escape me. I'm indebted to you. Blessings and love to you." ~ Lynne H.

"This is a beautiful bit of writing! I love your way with words. Such a gorgeous soul shines through with each one. Thank you for writing." ~ Joy P.

"I would like to say to you, dearest River... you are truly special. Thank you and thank you even more for this journey." ~ Gillian T.

"Loved, loved, LOVED this post! Thanks for putting into words... the art of food! You inspired me to go to my local city market this weekend, despite the heat predicted, where I hope to find a bit of magic and mindfulness. As always, thank you for sharing, it made my day... again." ~ SH

"Your words cause a stirring of the artistic... and a need to live more mindfully and creatively. Thank you so very much." ~ JWP

"As usual, this post resonated strongly with me and comes at the perfect time. Your writings always seem to be speaking directly to my soul, exactly what I need to hear... you so eloquently voice what is so very jumbled in my head. Your words never fail to move me. Thank you!" ~ Theresa R.

"As a late-comer to Soul Artist Journal, I have looked forward to receiving your posts. I so enjoy them, as a reminder to ponder the simple joys of life..."
~ Christine S.

"Thank you so much again for sharing your heart and reopening mine."
~ Pamela B.

"Beautiful, as always. Such a gift to read your words." ~ Randy L.

"I just read your latest piece, 'Patience and Wild Things'... GORGEOUS!"
~ Mary T.

"Please... keep the words flowing so eloquently, so poetically and help more folks find their way back home to their deepest inner soul space..." ~ Mare C.

"This is a beautiful, vulnerable, perfect reminder. Thank you for writing and sharing this piece so sprawled out and open." ~ L.C.

For Robert, the blue-eyed boy in a frumpy green coat who became the most noble knight upon the field.

Also by L.R. Heartsong:

The Bones & Breath:
A Man's Guide to Eros, the Sacred Masculine, and the Wild Soul
[Nautilus Award winner]

To Kneel and Kiss the Earth: Inspiration from the Soul Artist
Journal

A Life for the Senses: Return to the Soul Artist Journal

Ordinary Sacred

Farewell to the Soul Artist Journal

L.R. Heartsong

Award–winning author of *The Bones & Breath:*
A Man's Guide to Eros, the Sacred Masculine, and the Wild Soul

Hearthside Press ❧ Bend, Oregon

Hearthside Press
PO Box 8507
Bend, Oregon 97708

Cover image by the author
Cover and interior design by Katie Elizabeth Boyer Clark
(www.katielizabeth.com)
Author photo by Rae Huo

First edition: 2022

Printed in the USA

ISBN: 978-0-578-54189-1 (paperback)

Contents

🐦 🐦 🐦

🐦 🐦 🐦

Preface

We come to things when ready for them. Following publication of *A Life for the Senses* (2020), the second compilation from the Soul Artist Journal, whenever I received requests or enquiries from readers whether further volumes would be forthcoming, my answer was *no.* Irrespective that dozens of suitable posts remained in the archives (the Journal's five-year span resulted in more than two hundred and twenty-five installments), I felt finished with my initial e-column launched in 2012. The SAJ was the past and I had little, if any, desire to revisit or return to what I penned as an emerging writer, entertaining or nourishing as it may still be.

Journal posts generally followed a certain format: sharing my personal, sensate experience—often barefoot in nature, or in the kitchen as a Paris-trained chef—in an attempt to offer *soulful nourishment.* A commendable motivation, I think, and as stated in the Introduction(s) to previous volumes, the weekly writing became a steady practice in showing up at the page come hell or high water, my *giveaway* from the heart.

Since the SAJ days, having traveled down the road several years, my perspective has widened. I would like to think this is *wisdom*, of course, but maybe it's just a bit of maturity. (Alas that the two aren't always connected.) Whatever the case, these dear posts are not what I'd write today, if simply because the view is *so* much larger from where I stand now.

Looking back, despite the self-oriented focus (endemic to personal blogs, I daresay), what strikes me is an inherent goodness and beauty in so many of the offerings. Again and again, the words were sweeping brushstrokes upon a canvas of the *ordinary sacred*—reflecting the Journal's unofficial tagline, "celebrating a life for the senses... and the ordinary sacred."

As relayed in the Preface to the second SAJ compilation, a desire to continue sharing soulful nourishment propelled me to deliver that follow-up offering of collected posts. As the world spins on—sorely divided, dark, and challenging for so many people, with "heavy-handed" almost the norm—some *lightness* would be a gift indeed. Contemplating a third SAJ volume, a wish to share *goodness* is what brings me to assemble this final retrospective.

So here we have it: a third installment to complete the Soul Artist Journal trilogy. Each book aims to give a glimpse into the richness of a deeply embodied life when senses are cast wide, welcoming and celebrating the otherwise mundane moment(s).

Half-jokingly, I often refer to the SAJ compilations as "my tea and scones books"— perfect for picking up and flipping open to a random selection, a post or two read with a cup of something nice (whatever one chooses to imbibe), and just as easily set down. No big commitment or arduous effort, just a graceful, nourishing pause in the day or perhaps before bed. Any time, really. Some delectable morsels to savor. A bit of everyday magic, of sorts, or, as I've put it elsewhere, a nod to the re-enchantment of everyday life.

Friend, what a privilege to offer one last serving of literary tea biscuits, scones, or *madeleines* (such choice!) from the Soul Artist Journal. Mirroring the previous volumes with a cross-section of categories and all years of the e-column, in making my selections I held in soft focus the *ordinary sacred*—a golden thread woven through a great many of the writings. Other themes could have been chosen, but it seems right to conclude the trilogy on this note echoing the Journal's heartbeat.

Sequels seldom live up to the original; however, sitting with what I've gathered, just possibly, here is an exception. An offering that feels both timely and timeless; something delightful that inspires and uplifts. Join me in the pages that follow for a last look backward, where I invite you into the soul-nourishing landscape—a *soulscape*—of one life deliberately inhabited. One that, weekly, I endeavored to share as a humble offering of grace and graciousness.

Gentle reader, may this little book land in your heart. And wherever the winding road leads, I hope your journey is a soulful celebration of life's ordinary moments. We are only here a short while, after all.

L.R. Heartsong
Early spring, 2022

Introduction: About the Journal
{From the SAJ website}

We all need inspiration on our journey. For nearly five years, the Soul Artist Journal explored weekly the art of living a meaningful, connected existence that cultivates a sense of well-being. Though the posts were diverse, there was an underlying theme: *how do we nourish the soul?*

What does it mean to be a Soul Artist? The SAJ articles offered reflections on those little, ordinary human moments of the day: a cup of tea, a fading flower in the garden, puttering in the kitchen, a stroll through the neighborhood or along a wild riverbank. Each entry, in differing ways, extolled the importance of opening our senses and heart to the living field of intelligence we are continually bathed in. How does the moment *feel?* What is on our plate to share? How can we nurture and befriend the body as ecstatic resource for a life of vitality and well-being? What is ours to bring to this multidimensional relationship—with place, humans, earth's denizens, and planet? What is the Deep Imagination? And how do we heal and *evolve?*

The Journal traveled its own spiral and arc, varying in length and tone over the years. Yet it always sought to illuminate conscious living and embodiment, gratitude, creativity, personal authenticity and transformation, seasonal food, natural beauty, and a sensual connection with nature and earth.

In short, these writings celebrate a life for the senses... and the ordinary sacred.

Perhaps pour yourself a cup of something, and then sit somewhere comfortable and quiet. Inhale a couple of deep breaths, sweeping aside the noisy voices and demands of the day—if only for now—and take a little journey for your soul.

Welcome, traveler.

❧ ❧ ❧

Author's Note

My years of living in England changed me, both in subtle and more definite ways; mostly for the better, I think. That said, I'm really not sure I can get through a day without proper teatime (and biscuits, thank you).

In written words, the lingering UK influence is evidenced by a preference for British spellings, though I generally keep to the American "z" instead of an "s" (e.g. "actualize" versus *actualise,* "civilization" rather than *civilisation,* etc.). Further, the Queen's English rules of grammar (spaces around en-dashes, for instance, and single apostrophe versus quotation marks) feel and look more 'right' to me than those set forth by that American gospel, The Chicago Manual of Style. And I am rather fond of qualifiers *(some, very, rather, too, much)* which the Brits adore and employ regularly in speaking and writing, but current American grammar regards as superfluous and cluttered.

Regularly, I notice my inconsistency of choice(s), switching back and forth, occasionally even within the same post, as if I'm a hybrid engine. At times I have thought to comb through past writings, tidying them up, assigning a passport and nationality once and for all. I tell myself that most of my readers are American, and if I ever landed a literary agent or New York publisher, an editor would certainly force the home rules.

In the end, I have not made such changes, nor committed to either shore of the Atlantic. Truly, I'm not trying to be pretentious or affected. Even beyond writing, in matters of food, clothing, language, and general tastes, my style is an amalgam of Old World and new. And somehow this feels strangely right, reflecting who I am as a wandering, soulful nomad, gathering bits of what I like from here and there, discarding the rest.

So, onwards we go, and we shall *savour* the *flavour* of *favourites* with *colourful neighbours* and whatnot. And I will always have a *garden* rather than a yard.

❧ ❧ ❧

Writing for the Love of Food, Nature, and Soul
(January, 2016)

Sometimes I think I should simply write about food. Forget this soul-based stuff, let's just go back to the kitchen, shall we?

Yes, I could easily keep adding posts to the Slow Food category on my website. Cook that I am, the kitchen is where you'll find me every single day, crafting something for dinner whether simple or elaborate (usually the former). While I'm not food-obsessed, and certainly don't consider myself a "foodie," I *am* frequently musing on what's to eat, the things I might like to combine and create. To taste—either for myself or to share. Really, that is what led me to culinary school in Paris and my former work as a private chef: a deep love of preparing simple, beautiful fare that honors the earth it came from.

It's a mixed bag, this Soul Artist Journal: a bit of this, a splash of that, a dollop of something else. Perhaps it's not unlike the *box scheme* of farm-fresh vegetables delivered weekly to the doorstep when I lived in England, never quite sure what's going to turn up from one week to the next. Honestly, how many onions can one use? Or potatoes and carrots? And though the unifying thread in these posts is always *soul*, a curious diversity has existed from the beginning, because prior to becoming a chef, I was a bodyworker, counselor, and healer. (Still am, actually.)

In 2012, recently returned from years of living in Europe, looking to attract a publisher for my book manuscript, I began building an author's platform by launching the Riverspeak podcast (now defunct, despite ongoing requests to bring it back) and this Soul Artist Journal. What began as merely a means to an end, steadily shifted and drew me in, becoming a weekly practice that changed me for the better; not simply for the focus of writing itself and an evolving "voice," but because these posts go forth weekly, there is a certain letting go of perfectionism, or even any attachment to outcome. Some installments are better than others, so be it. Knowing that the posts must be live on Sunday morning come Hell or high water, the Journal has instilled in me both a sense of discipline and devotion.

During the past four years, the maturing SAJ finally found its authentic voice with "celebrating a life for the senses" (though I didn't adopt that as a logo or tagline until quite recently). And I've come to realize that so often what I'm writing about, inviting people to make room for in their lives, is the *ordinary sacred*.

My reading interests tend to hover around nature, cuisine and wine, France, and *personal evolution*, and lately I've been following a couple of award-winning food blogs. Yet despite the occasional temptation to settle in comfortably and simply write about being in the kitchen, to exalt the rustic, local, seasonal fare I love to prepare, I figure that the world doesn't need another food blogger—probably not even a French-trained, barefoot, nature-boy attuned to the subtle art of nourishing the soul.

Too, there's the very real matter when I glance out the front windows of this California cottage near the sea, observing the coastal light cascading through spiraling, wind-raked limbs of the great Monterey cypress (the Grandmother, I call her). For a moment my breath catches, seeing the bare winter garden suddenly illuminated as a living, breathing poem, and I deeply ache to share *that* beauty.

Whenever I'm rambling upon the wild seashore or amid whispering trees, charmed by the chattering discourse of a family of red-capped acorn woodpeckers in a gnarled silver oak, I want to share *that too*. Similarly with the bright green blades of irises stabbing up from dark soil, seemingly everywhere in the neighborhood where I walk my two English Whippets, the Sussex Duo. Or my childlike joy that the little winged ones have finally discovered the Arts & Crafts bronze bird feeder I received from my beloved at winter solstice (my chosen holiday).

I yearn to relate the wordless grace of greeting the dawn with an open heart and a cup of tea as I do each morning, feeling expansion in my chest at the twinkling inspiration of a diamond star in the periwinkle sky. And I wish for you to meet the sly red fox in an open, green field, each surprised by the other. Or a deepening into the quietude of writing with a trusty Paris fountain pen by candlelight in a ramshackle cottage at the edge of a continent, hearing the rumbling low voice of the ocean like an ancient chant at night. Daily, I long to give you the cool of grey stones and sweet, damp earth beneath bare soles, the briny taste of the air, and the alluring perfume of ripe, organic strawberries at a farmers market.

Because each of these things—and a thousand more—in its own way offers an antidote for the ailments of life, the tiring crush and electric hum, those lingering troubles and heartaches that beset us all in one form or another. *Healing* and *nourishment* of the soul sort, that's really what I write about.

How easy it is to lose touch of the tactile, goodness of our days, especially when beauty seems distant and mostly forgotten or ignored in a harried rush. Yet beauty exists *everywhere*. Most of us are simply not paying attention. And in both the heart and senses, too many of us are closed like a fist rather than a hand held open in giving.

Every day, I am seduced by sensual moments of ordinary, heart-fluttering beauty that I love to offer forward, just as I would something from my kitchen, handed to you on a simple, handmade plate.

Be open, my friend.

If you read this journal at all regularly, you know that I'm an old fashioned, mostly quiet fellow who repeatedly encourages others to slow down, to unplug from a wired existence, and to dilate their senses. *Taste. See. Listen. Smell. Feel.* I remind people (myself included) to relish the pleasures of life with a wild heart steeped in gratitude, urging us all to savor the precious gifts of being fully human, even amid the challenges. Especially then. Life is not always art but certainly there exists an *art* and *soul* to living—to cooking, eating, writing, walking and sitting, dancing, friendship, making love—and it is a worthy goal to live gracefully, both in abundance and in need.

Some of you would like more food-based posts, and I would dearly love cook some up. Others hope for more nature-based writing and creative inspiration, and I want to deliver you that, too. Yet I'm afraid it's like dinner at our house, where I can't really predict what is going to appear on the table; it simply depends on what's local and in season, what I fancy at the market and caught my eye, or whatever *feels* right somehow.

Perhaps what I can give you regularly is this: a nod towards the re-enchantment of everyday life. For when our senses and hearts are ajar, and if we are paying attention, we discover that a subtle sense of magic *still* inhabits the world, hidden within familiar forms. There's goodness in that.

Come, pull up a chair. Gather round our well-traveled dining table of darkly polished wood. Perhaps I'll light a fire on the hearth or, at the very least, a couple of hand-dipped beeswax candles. Let me pour you a cup of tea in a blue and white porcelain cup from England, with some sweet nibbles on a plate between us. Let's sit and talk like old friends about our deep longing—the hunger we feel—for a dear place and food for the soul, for healing and magic, love and personal evolution, and for a connection to something larger. Much larger.

Gentle reader, as the days fly away, let us savor and share the best of what we have. And in a prayer for the world, may all be fed and nourished deeply.

❦ ❦ ❦

Patience and Wild Things

(September, 2014)

How impatient we are as a species.

In the morning light, I stood on a rocky shore called Granite Beach; "beach" a highly inaccurate misnomer in this case, rather an arc of sea cove populated with thousands of small, rounded granite stones washed up against the low cliffs.

I had chosen to spend a significant portion of my morning at Point Lobos State Reserve, just south of Carmel-by-the-Sea, not far from the little artist cottage I rent. The Reserve derives its name not from any wolves ("lobos") that once roamed the area but rather from the colonizing Spaniards' name for this rocky spear of land – *el punto de los lobos del mar* – where the barking of resident sea lions could be heard in the rocky coves. (In old Spanish they were called *sea wolves* rather than sea lions.)

A sky of flatly hammered tin pressed down upon a restless sea. After roaming barefoot on various trails along the water's edge, stopping every now and then to converse with some tree, bush, or bird, I made my way to the sheltered cove of Granite Beach, descending on a dirt track through a small, narrow ravine that smelled of resinous pine, dry brush and summer dust, and then emerged on the rocky expanse of shoreline.

The water was a deep, still emerald that shimmered and lapped softly near my feet with a gently lulling chant. How curious that only a few small coves away, either north or south, the Pacific waves rolled and crashed with gusto, yet where I stood all was gentleness and tranquility.

For a while I watched the black cormorants on the far arm of shore, scrambling along the cliffside to their nests or launching into the air only to alight in the blue-green waters and paddle about or dive for a meal. On several large rocks, silkily plump harbor seals had emerged from their submerged world of swaying kelp forests, resting awkwardly exposed in poses that looked decidedly uncomfortable. Seemingly, they have sufficient blubber that the rough, uneven ridges don't feel sharp, but my body exhaled a sigh of relief that I don't sleep on such a harsh, unwelcoming bed.

Wordlessly, I drank it all in: the wealth of interesting round stones underfoot, the various seabirds and dozing seals, the rugged beauty of windswept Monterey cypresses upon the low cliffs, the murmuring voice of the ocean breeze and waves gently breaking at my feet. Yet my attention was most drawn by a grey heron standing on a shifting mass of floating brown sea kelp some twenty yards offshore. Subtle, balancing movements sequenced through the long legs and graceful body as he rode the gentle rise and fall of thickly glistening fronds – all while poised in stillness, scanning the jade waters for food. Slender, elegant neck craned forward, the creature peered into the tangles of seaweed with only the occasional, slightest turn of head; a model of poise and anticipatory movement, ready to unwind dramatically into fully expressed motion at any second.

Patiently he waited, as handfuls of sunlight diamonds flashed across the water's surface, while in my own musculature and breath I could feel the winged one's readiness.

Gulls cried in the air. Cormorants dove and then took again to the sky. The seals occasionally made loud, snorting exhales (perhaps they were farts, I don't know) as they shifted their ungainly positions. Aimlessly, I wandered up and down the rocky shoreline that shifted and rolled beneath my bare feet, occasionally stooping down to lift and examine some rounded stone that caught my eye, turning its cool, ancient being over in my warm palm. Yet my gaze kept returning to the heron on the floating kelp in his watchful pose of stillness.

As so many times before, once again I was struck by how *patient* every wild thing must be as it waits or hunts for its next meal. And how impatient humankind is – myself, included.

Irrespective of hunger rumbling in the belly, or exhaustion from a night of little sleep as winds howl, other beings embody a willingness to wait in a way that we do not. I consider my own impatience when I am unfed and/or tired, of the countless instances of wanting something and wanting it *now*; all the times when *in a few hours* or, perish the thought, *tomorrow*, simply won't do. Breath is shallow and my gut constricts with angst and anxiety – such a very far cry from the heron's watchful poise. What I do really know about *waiting?*

How restless, fretful, and agitated we are. How unaccustomed – unwilling – to simply wait, to let things come to us when they may. Ours is a society hooked on nearly instant gratification, when the information, entertainment, or distraction we want is merely a few clicks away. Sex, even. Our impulse purchases can arrive tomorrow via express overnight shipping. We fuss if the Internet connection is slow, or when we have to stand in a queue at the grocery store or post office. Most modern lives move at blazing speed (when not snarled in traffic) both day and night, a pace utterly disconnected from the natural world from which we emerged.

Carefully navigating the shifting stones, frowning that this expedition along the shoreline was probably not good for my slowly healing foot, I moved on from the jade cove with the hunting heron and snorting seals. Allurement drew me to wander north towards the lone, great standing stone on a bluff I spied from a distance – something Old World in its stature and demeanor, like it belonged on a verdant plain in Ireland or Britain. As if it were reaching out from the realm of spirits, calling to me or its far distant kin, I felt compelled to answer and lay hands upon it, so I headed in that direction.

After the sunny weekend just past, the Reserve mobbed with visitors and cars parked along both sides of the road for a mile, Point Lobos was pleasantly uncrowded on this cloudy Tuesday morning. Walking the empty trails, I was nearly alone for human company. At one point, in my usual curious way, I stopped to examine something along the path and noticed my bare footprints in the dust; rounded and singularly different from all the imprints of hiking boots and rubber soles that had passed this way and left rigidly geometric but fleeting stamps.

One of these things is not like the others, I mused. The observation struck me as a fittingly appropriate self-description. Humourous, even.

The well-trafficked artery of coastal Highway 1 lay just a short distance away but, as I wandered, the manmade din of the world, cars, and paved roads seemed far removed. Contentedly, I ambled like a lover, seduced by the palette of nature's colours that greeted my eye, from the flaming red of the Poison Oak seemingly everywhere to the long shaggy beards of sage green moss adorning the Monterey cypress trees, which are indigenous to this very point of land. Green conifers against the backdrop of pewter clouds, the pale scrub and tawny grasses studded profusely with purple flowers, the shifting hues of sea that mirrored a changeling sky above, my wild soul was bathed sweetly in tones of coastal beauty.

Nearly an hour later, returning from the great monolith on the rocky bluff, passing the jade cove of Granite Beach below me, I looked down and halted. The heron was still perched on the kelp in the same spot. Waiting. Watching. From the bluff's edge, I bowed to him.

"Blessed be, patient one," I said aloud.

My own hunger was stirring, urging me on toward home for a tasty lunch. Accompanying that rumbling in the gut was my own desire to put some of my thoughts and observations – scrawled into my little black journal as I sat and walked – into a more coherent and articulated form (for this very post). And I found myself mentally going over the checklist of things I needed to accomplish in the afternoon. Though if I really considered whether my list held deeper merit, a good deal of the work that called was just habit and routine – it didn't *have* to be done today. Once again, I recognized the ingrained cultural impetus toward *doing* rather than simply *being* – a chronic, acute case of "hurry-busy disease." Most of us are tightly wrapped in busy agendas, rushing here and there, chasing and grasping at desires when, truthfully, very little of such busy-ness is relevant in the larger scheme. (Simply look at the Earth from space and perspective changes radically.)

Sometimes I'm better at waiting than other times, and comparatively I'm a fairly patient soul. Today, the graceful grey heron humbled me as he balanced atop the floating kelp, teacher that he was. Reminding me. Thank you, elegant Master.

Lately, I have felt frustrated with the slow turning wheels in the publishing world, anxious for my first book to roll off the press onto shelves and greet the world. Yet does it really matter when it arrives? Not so much. Too, I wrestle with impatience in relaunching my coaching and men's work, wanting doors to open and meaningful connections to appear before they are actually *ready* to manifest, in that the forthcoming book holds the key.

Patience, River.

Despite the stunning beauty that surrounds me where I dwell, often I forget where I really am; swept up in the tasks of the day, losing myself in a hurry to get *somewhere*, eager to put this particular passage of time behind me. My ego's time schedule versus that of the Larger Story are quite often at odds, just another laugh in the ongoing Cosmic Joke (which, by the way, is *always* on us). Repeatedly I am given the opportunity to *let go of my agenda*. Simply wait. Step outside and breathe the unconditioned air. But oh, how difficult that can be when feeling tired, hungry or simply *wanting*.

One could argue that *patience* isn't the primary thing we might learn from nature, for plenty of *industrious* examples exist to inspire us – the bees, ants, hummingbirds, and all manner of creatures that work ceaselessly. Fair enough. However, I think in terms of *balance* we might learn more from the patient ones than those who are ever busy. Actually, I would offer that Nature offers myriad lessons to her wayward, disconnected, human children, especially regarding *relationship* and *interdependence*, diversity, and sustainability.

I'm still learning that life is a balance between *doing* and simply *being*. Realizing that value exists in learning to wait patiently, for certain things cannot be rushed. From the moment the spark of creation seeds the womb of possibility, a period of hidden gestation occurs. Things do not appear instantly, they must form. In a restless, impatient world shorn of mystery and meaning, blessed are those who learn to wait in beauty with expansive breath. Time is relative, subjective, and easily squandered – and the future moment we rush headlong to greet is not necessarily better than this one.

Gentle reader, here's hoping you can welcome a bit of patience in your day. Possibly your path will cross with something or someone – gnarled oak tree, round blue stone, shimmering body of water, bright oxtail daisy, a little yellow bird, the drifting clouds, a leafy and tenacious vine, or a gentle soul – reminding you that the *real world* (versus the artificial one about which we endlessly fuss and fret) moves and breathes and blossoms at a different pace altogether. Despite our seeming severance from nature, we remain part of that milieu, a natural and healing one, right down to a cellular level. A soul level, even. And there is a *much* larger story unfolding. Yes, indeed.

The season shifts, days growing shorter. Inhale a deep breath, my friend, tasting the subtle change in the air itself. Soften your jaw. Relax the shoulders. Whatever you may be waiting impatiently for or heatedly pursuing, choose something to savour in the moment with all your senses cast wide.

Here in the Northern Hemisphere, autumn is nearly on our doorstep. The turning inward begins once more, whether we like it or not. Just possibly, we can greet it with an open heart and mind, welcoming whatever it may bring.

And may we each learn patience like a graceful, great heron.

„ „ „

The Dawn Summons

(December, 2013)

The harsh sonic blast jolted me awake in a panic.

In predawn darkness, the loud electronic siren in the house roused me instantly from deep dreaming. Confused, I thought it was the newly installed burglar alarm in this Hawaii rental (there have been a rash of break-ins in the neighborhood). My beloved is away from the islands and I am alone with our English Whippets, so I leapt out of bed and dashed naked into the hallway where the electronic keypad glowed in darkness.

My still-dreaming brain struggled to wake up and make full sense of the piercing noise stabbing my eardrums. Standing in the hallway, squinting at the keypad with my nearly blind eyes, I saw green lights, not red. As the dogs ran about the house in their own state of distress, I realized that the electronic scream wasn't nearly loud enough to be the house alarm; instead, the smoke detectors were blaring in the office and the kitchen simultaneously.

"Damn it!" I cursed loudly.

The fire alarms have repeatedly gone off in this rented Kailua residence for no apparent reason, nearly always in the middle of the night. Now another two were screaming forth simultaneously without any smoke or fire. The alarms are hotwired into the house electrical system with a battery backup; they should emit a chirp when a battery needs replacing rather than activating their sonic warning.

Still naked, I stood on the office chair while the siren blasted me and I attempted to unscrew the round, plastic device. Removing the battery failed to stop the high-volume assault, and just as with the one in my office a week ago, the wires are snugly fitted into a plastic component that must be pried loose. It took a few painfully delirious, still half-asleep minutes, but I managed to get both alarms disconnected and blessedly silenced.

No fire, no smoke. Surely all four alarms cannot need a new battery within ten days of each other? Either we have a short-circuit in the wiring or an ethereal spirit visitor is attempting to get my attention in a very rude fashion.

In the kitchen, I climbed down from the granite countertop, ears still ringing.

Outside, an island world remained cloaked in velvety darkness, and I stood for a moment, groggily considering the available options. Squinting to read the clock digits glowing on the stove, noting it was five o'clock, with a sigh, resigned myself that I would have to remain awake. For me, waking anytime near five means the night is essentially over; I might as well get up because I won't fall back asleep. Moreover, I need to eat to stabilize my blood sugar or soon I'll be wobbly, a poor way to begin the day.

Lifting the glass dome covering a stack of gluten-free scones baked the night previous (primarily ground flax seeds, ground almonds, coconut flour, a low-glycemic sweetener, and deliciously spiked with ginger and dried cranberries), I set a confection on a small plate – but ate it standing up in the kitchen, still somewhat in a muddle. Meanwhile, with the sonic crisis over and too early for their breakfast, the Sussex Duo headed back to the warmth of bed.

"Sorry, boys," I apologized, feeling sorry for their sensitive ears and the high-decibel assault that so distressed them.

For a moment, I pondered whether these repeated alarms in the middle of the night and wee hours of morning might be caused by a disincarnate entity seeking my attention. Or some other mysterious element I don't understand. Much as I've tried to shut the door on being *spooky*, I still seem to dwell at the threshold between worlds, and paranormal events are a regular occurrence in my life.

Accepting that sleep was over, I filled the cobalt blue kettle with water and placed it on the stove to heat for tea. In short order, early as it was, I would sit at the dining room table with a steaming cup of fragrant brew and settle into the day's work of editing the book's conclusion. From another room, I fetched my notebook and the printed pages, along with my cracked but indispensable fountain pen from Paris with which I write everything – every post, every chapter – longhand. (I'm a very old fashioned soul.)

Before tea and work, however, outside to greet the dawn.

After pulling on hemp yoga pants and t-shirt to save naked flesh from the ever-present mosquitoes, and deactivating the house general alarm at the keypad, I slid open one of the glass doors in the living room and stepped barefoot outside into the warm, humid darkness. Beyond the *lanai*, crossing the wet grass, I threaded my way to the edge of the rear lawn between the two great sentinel trees; a venerable mango and an old poinciana I call the Prayer Tree. There, I gazed up at clouded, tropical mountains looming close at hand, opening my heart and senses wide.

I stood for a while, savouring the relative quietude and moist air. The dawn chorus of birds had not yet begun, and the rich stillness was broken only by a symphony of crickets, feral chickens crowing in the ravine below, and the distant hum of early commuters on the Pali Highway. In the darkness, I offered prayers of gratitude and intentions for the day, allowing my body to sway and stretch with easy, gentle movements, slowly coming to fully awake.

Unbidden, a favourite song of mine surfaced in my mind. Since living in southern Spain, "Silence," sung by Georgia-born singer Lizz Wright, has been my *dawn song*, offered forth to the 'other-than-human' world when I greet a day's arrival beneath the sky. I suspect that when this life is over, "Silence" will be one of a dozen tunes that rise up from my body like wispy blue smoke, carrying the very essence of my being.

Standing at the edge of the ravine, softly I begin to sing aloud.

Have you heard the silent night?
The Earth is always singing
praises of the morning sun
even before morning...
And the whole world is singing of
its beauty all day long...
And even the quiet dark
that silence is a song...
Weep not for the day of grey
for the heavens are not weeping...
Roses are still red and gay
they are even blooming...
And the whole world is singing of
its beauty all day long...
And even the quiet dark
that silence is a song,
that silence is a song...

Quietude again wrapped around me like a shawl, and I recalled another morning a couple of years ago, near the end of our time in Andalucía, Spain. Alone in the old stone farmhouse, I was woken in predawn darkness by a storm forcing open the windows and balcony doors in multiple rooms. A great commotion. After closing things up, and gathering the pages of book manuscript blown all around my writing room, I made my way downstairs, where I unlocked the heavy wooden doors and went outside to stand on the broad gravel terrace, looking out over the *campo* and olive groves still in shadows. As if it had never been, no trace of the storm existed other than the wet stones and the smell of fresh, hard rain. I couldn't see the distant wedge of the Mediterranean, just a few bright stars of early morning, but as I opened my senses to that ancient landscape, once again I heard it: the Song of the World – the very sound of Creation *singing*.

Twice before I had experienced this seemingly divine grace: once in England just before dawn, and at home in Andalucía one evening at dusk. A jubilant exultation from the trees and Earth in a suprasonic audio range beyond normal hearing, perceptible only in a mode of highly expanded awareness. A celebration for the beauty of life itself, exactly like described in Lizz Wright's "Silence"… but *wordless*. Both episodes shook me to my core, rearranging my entire worldview of reality as if shorn by a bolt of exquisite lightning. Standing on the terrace in southerly Spain in early morning darkness, summoned by a storm, and after singing to the coming dawn, I heard it once more – all of Creation in chorus. My heart swelled, my entire being expanded, and tears rolled down my cheeks to bless the earth at my feet. It felt like a gift from the Universe, and I will carry the memory to the end of my days.

The story of that dawn awakening as a sort of mysterious summons, opened the final chapter of my original manuscript, including the song by Lizz Wright. Standing in the island darkness, bare soles in wet grass, I wondered whether some connection existed between that morning two years ago and this one. There are some similarities – alone in the house, partner away, woken early by unexplained occurrences, working on the conclusion of a book – but if a thread exists, it isn't yet obvious to me.

At the rim of the ravine, I listened for the Song of the World, quietly hoping, but all that greeted me in the darkness were familiar sounds of feral chickens in the tangled greenery and distant cars on the highway.

I turned towards the house and slowly walked back to the *lanai* where I wiped my grassy feet on the outdoor mat, and then stepped inside for morning tea. Though still enfolded by darkness, the day had been properly met with prayers, gratitude, and intention. A song, no less. Time now to settle in to my tasks.

Perhaps it is simply some faulty wiring that set off the smoke detectors this morning. Or maybe we have a mischievous spirit in the house. Whether I was somehow summoned by otherworldly forces to rise earlier than normal and come outdoors to sing to the trees, earth, and sky, who can say. What I know is that my work today has flowed in a mostly effortless and voluminous fashion for which I am truly grateful. For the first time in my life, I have a publisher's deadline for my writing (it looms at the end of this month when the edited manuscript is due), and I am determined to accomplish as much as possible in these ten days of solitude, immersing myself in the task at hand.

Yet beyond current efforts of writing or editing, I'm really a Soul Artist; routinely engaged in polysensory communion with the 'other-than-human' world, seeking to offer something of value to the web of life. I hope these weekly posts convey some measure of that.

Gentle reader, here's hoping that Grace embraces you in its unique way today. May your breath feel easy and full. In our noisy world, perhaps you can find a bit of silence and savor it, like a honeybee sips nectar from an enticing flower. Do something that *nourishes* your soul. My conviction is that the real purpose of life is to offer the singular beauty of oneself, to carry that which *only you* can bring to the world, and share it wholeheartedly. Unabashedly. I share this extensively in my forthcoming book, *The Bones and Breath*, that modest as one's existence may seem, each life we touch affects countless others; we are all interconnected, and *everything is relationship*.

Don't go back to sleep.

❧ ❧ ❧

Freeing the Tiger

(March, 2015)

The growl emerges somewhere at the back of my throat, something wild and unfriendly lurking in the shadows of a damp, darkened cave.

I continue to summon the sound, pushing it forward with breath and support from my respiratory diaphragm, and like a fire fed with fuel and oxygen, it grows quickly in both intensity and ferocity. The corners of my mouth turn up in a snarl, something decidedly savage trying to break free.

It began harmlessly enough with a bit of easy movement to some music to wake up my body, which felt heavy and dense as an Irish bog in wintertime. As I moved and stretched, finding the tight places in my muscles and joints, hearing and feeling the old, limiting stories, I began to add sound—long vowels extended into tones to awaken the voice. After a while, feeling warm and loosened, I let movement settle to a standstill and focused simply on the "sounding," supporting it fully with breath.

Ohm... ohm.... ohm...

The volume increases. For a brief moment, I fret about people walking by the cottage, or my neighbor across the camellia hedge, imagining them hearing strange sounds emanating from this little house behind the weathered fence beneath the grandmother Monterey cypress. Once again, the familiar patterns of containment wish to keep me small, quiet, and polite.

Don't be too loud, admonishes the inner Good Boy Scout.

Oh, bugger off, I retort silently. Don't hold back. Who cares who hears?

I begin to tone more loudly, a resonant *ohm* that enlivens my entire body with a deep vibration. It feels pleasurable, both energizing and expansive, as if all the locked wooden doors inside me have been suddenly flung open to the bright light of a spring morning. In a more complex manner than through physical motor movement alone, my bodysoul tingles and comes awake with the sound. It is freeing, like taking off clothing that fits too tightly and being pleasantly naked.

Allowing it, the vocal toning grows richer, fuller and more resonant.

Experimenting with different pitches and octaves, exploring the lower range in particular, the growl unexpectedly begins—initiating with a subtle tension in jaw muscles, a clamped movement seeking to release. Curious about the sensation, I allow my mandible to begin to move slightly to the right, noticing an immediate shift in affect and sensation that ensues.

The resonant, growling *ohm* transforms into something more guttural, ugly, and raw. My abdominals tighten like a fist clenched, ready to strike or crush whatever is held. Freed by a modest movement, the corners of my mouth curl up further and the snarl intensifies, while simultaneously a contingent of facial muscles unlock as my neck begins to pivot and rotate. For a short while, the rigidity in jaw and face feels welded in place like an iron mask, heavy in its weight.

The motion of my head, the movement of unlocked jaw bones, and the loud growling are conspiring to release something feral and too long bound. A tremulous ripple of electricity grows in strength, coursing through my entire body, animating me to greater movement and freedom. Unbidden, a wave of anger rises up like a hot, searing flash of red, and I can feel it secured in the steel trap of my maw.

I surrender fully to sound and movement, unleashing my restraint and any timid self-consciousness or shame. My face contorts into a hideous, raging howl—along with a palpable, extreme tension aching to be freed—and I roar with all my might, filling the room with deafening sound.

The seemingly tame tiger captive at the zoo lunges and strikes out, a hungry man-eater, devouring his unsuspecting feeder alive with flashing yellow fangs. The taste of warm blood intoxicates. A quiet and gentle man, I morph into something wild and unrestrained, a hungry werewolf beneath the silver coin of a full moon. Swept up, I cast away any remaining concerns about being heard and surrender fully to the loud howling and facial contortions that now have a life of their own.

The background music I was initially moving and listening to has disappeared in the unexpected storm. A river unleashed, my body burns and trembles with rage and power that I have long secured away in rigid tissues, fascia, bones, and shallow breath. Movement uncurls rapidly in the core like a glistening ebony cobra and I yield to it, allowing my body to sway freely. Spine undulates, snakelike, sending my entire frame into wave upon wave of oscillations as voice transforms from human to animal. I hold nothing back, letting myself writhe, kick, and explode with expressive movement and unrestrained kinetic power.

The embodied eruption of sound and emotion lasts about five minutes, utterly consuming me. Slowly, the snarling and dramatic movement abate. Emerging from the whitewater rapids, my bodysoul slides into an eddy of gently moving, quieter waters. This unforeseen tempest has ravaged the landscape, leaving the throat roughened, tender and raw, and my voice distinctly hoarse—like a smoker after a night of too many cigarettes, or a rock star after belting for hours in the stadium concert. The sound that emerges now is much lower in tone, richer, and full. Larger somehow.

Standing motionless, gazing out the front windows at the small enclosed world of the front garden beneath the great Monterey cypress, I scan down my body with interoceptive awareness. Every cell reverberates with a gentle, humming current and sense of expansion.

More than human, I am an open grassy field with the wind rippling through in waves of flashing silver green.

Face, neck and shoulders feel as if a layer of dense armor, previously camouflaged as skin and muscle, has been lifted away. I walk through the cottage, bare soles light upon the wooden floors, noting how my entire body feels almost ethereal as it moves, like I've dropped twenty pounds of weight. Subtle movement continues to ripple through my core and limbs like a somatic echo.

Even within the cottage walls, I notice a different sense of connection with my surroundings—more sensitive and intuitive, every sense heightened. Familiar boundaries between self and not-self have shifted, now permeable and diffuse. A changeling, I inhabit a sea of energy rather than the rigid, seemingly material world.

What would it take to live more fully this way every day? What is the part of me that censors such authentic power, and what do I gain from doing so?

How very deep and strong, the inner resistance keeping me safely in chains... until now.

Until now... because movement and sound are the antithesis of *restraint*.

Energized and awake, I seat myself at the old wooden table by the window to write, each breath open and full as I rest in an upholstered chair with well-worn cushions. My body is nothing but a prayer of fire and smoke. Unshackled and unrestrained. A wild soul, I am free to write honestly—dangerously, even—with a bold, unashamed voice.

What will I dare to bring forward?

❧ ❧ ❧

A Poem by Heart: A Soul Practice
(July, 2014)

In the early light, barefoot upon the earth and gazing across the lush tropical ravine, I repeated the poem aloud as a prayer. A new way to greet the morning, like a song without music, a few memorized stanzas as an offering to the holy.

Wiping wet soles upon the mat, back inside the house I opened a blue notebook on the glass and mahogany coffee table, and quietly read the lines again. Noting I had misspoken one of the words in the middle of the poem, I repeated the correct one a few times, invisibly turning it over in my palm like a smooth green stone, and tucked it away inside my heart.

❧

For some years now, I have kept a soft-sided blue folder stuffed full of meaningful, soul-centered poems by notable poets. I obtained it in the early days of my apprenticeship with an organization that leads contemporary "vision quests" and wilderness rites of passage, while training to be an "Underworld guide" as they call it—one who leads others into the depths of soul for personal transformation. Soulful poetry read or spoken to the group is a hallmark of their eco-depth psychology programs, for the imagery of such language speaks directly to the soul; it bypasses the logical, rational brain, stirs our feelings, and abducts us into deeper realms.

Though I dabbled with writing prosaic poems in early adulthood, I had been mostly estranged from poetry for many years. Certainly, I never encountered it read aloud in a meaningful way, despite that I had attended a few "open microphone" readings during my youthful Seattle days; mostly it felt like I didn't quite *get it*, perhaps because the poems being read didn't necessarily speak to me. Not until my "soul guide" apprenticeship—often seated on the earth in a circle of brave seekers in some wilderness location, enfolded by the alluring forms and forces of nature—did my heart open to the power of poetry. Time and place were right, so too were the poems. Everything finally clicked.

The cover of my dear blue notebook is slightly ripped, stained, and spotted. The pages within are folded over at corners to mark favorites, or adorned with little ribbons of yellow sticky notes. Many journeys it has traveled in my rucksack or carry bag, across oceans, even. I am familiar with all the poems and many of them feel like good friends—ones whose lines or stanzas I know intimately from reading and hearing them over and over. Through the years, I have added to the collection by typing up and printing out poems that resonate with me, tucking them into the front or rear pocket of the tattered folder.

Sometimes, I will simply open the collection to a page at random and read what is there, speaking it aloud to the silence. Occasionally to friends or loved ones. Back when I led men's groups, each session always began with a soul-infused poem to help participants drop into their bodies in a conscious, *feeling* way.

ᘓ

Attending the Redwood Men's Conference near Mendocino in May, my favorite element of the weekend was how a number of men stepped forward and spoke poems aloud by memory. Some of the gems offered I knew but many were new to me, and I was both humbled and inspired, for not even the familiar poems could I offer up without reading them on a page. *Wow, wow, wow...*

There is something visceral and powerful in a poem spoken aloud. Like hearing a well-told story, a timeless quality enfolds the listener. We pause. Our breath shifts and we *open* slightly in a non-habitual way. In an age of digital media where most people have become almost entirely focused upon our dominant, visual sense, listening to the spoken word cultivates a different channel among one's primary "windows of knowing." We're invited to pay attention, welcoming the words into our *bodysoul*, where they communicate directly to our feeling sense and heart. A spoken poem also reveals something about the speaker—they cared enough, were affected deeply enough by that poem to commit it to memory—we glimpse a bit of their soul through words.

ᘓ

Lately, I have been musing on the concept of *soul practice*—personal actions or rituals that deepen one into the realms of soul—considering and reinventing my own approach. As part of such reexamining, and inspired by the men's conference, I decided to begin committing favorite poems to memory; a dozen top contenders in the battered blue notebook springing immediately to mind. Learning a poem by heart feels like a rich vein of soul practice, and I like that it helps exercise my somewhat flabby muscles of memory and retention, too.

An embodied, soulful life is a conscious relationship with with body, mind, heart, and spirit.

Breath and somatic awareness are unsurpassed tools for this, but anything that shifts awareness into a mindful, observant state—such as a poem—can also be effective. The more frequently we descend from our heads into the body, and the more we recognize our patterns and responses as they play out (there is *always* a somatic component to every response), and to the extent that we open senses and heart to the relationships around us (physical environment, included), the more deeply we are *embodied* in a meaningful way.

The more fully embodied, the more we are *ensouled*. **Soul loves the body.** Indeed, as I have written in one of the chapters in *The Bones and Breath*, "Ensouling the Body," *the body is the soul's prayer*. More so than simply via transcendent or deep stillness, it is through expansive senses that we perceive the Mystery and our place in the interwoven relationship of creation.

A poem in the heart might effortlessly open and guide us, as well.

Listening to a musical composition, an attentive listener can often hear and feel the difference between a performance of simply playing the notes as marked, versus a musician(s) who has taken the score deep inside and allows music to emerge *through* them. The first is mechanical; the latter is artistic and truly musical. Listening to someone who has deeply inhabited a poem's soul can be similarly moving. Beyond mere memorization, there is a fluency of cadence and a sensitivity to silence—the spaces and silences surely as important as the words themselves. Possibly more so.

Thus for my own soul practice, I want to do more than simply memorize poems, rather I will welcome them into my heart and embody them to the best of my ability. Weighing which one I might first enter into ongoing relationship with, the choice was relatively easy. A lion's share of my favorites come from the pen of Pulitzer prize–winning, American poet, Mary Oliver, but one distinctly stood forward and invited me to dance.

Seated cross-legged on the floor, I opened the battered blue folder to the appropriate page, settled into my breath, and welcomed the familiar words to take up residence in my heart, as I repeated them slowly, again and again.

"The Summer Day"

Who made the world?
Who made the swan, and the black bear?
Who made the grasshopper?
This grasshopper, I mean—
the one who has flung herself out of the grass,
the one who is eating sugar out of my hand,
who is moving her jaws back and forth instead of up and down—
who is gazing around with her enormous and complicated eyes.
Now she lifts her pale forearms and thoroughly washes her face.
Now she snaps her wings open, and floats away.
I don't know exactly what a prayer is.
I do know how to pay attention, how to fall down
into the grass, how to kneel in the grass,
how to be idle and blessed, how to stroll through the fields,
which is what I have been doing all day.
Tell me, what else should I have done?
Doesn't everything die at last, and too soon?
Tell me, what is it you plan to do
with your one wild and precious life?

❧

This past month, each week I've been learning a new poem by heart. At odd
moments of the day—driving in the car, chopping vegetables in the kitchen,
standing in queue at the grocery store, walking the dogs at night—I find myself
repeating lines and stanzas to myself like a mantra or prayer. The act quietly
centers and invites me deeper into bones and breath, reminding me to relax tight
shoulders and breathe more fully into my belly; to waltz or tango with the images,
exploring their contours in a richer, more intimate way.

Another dozen poems are already earmarked in the battered blue folder, awaiting
me to sit with them—walk, breathe, twirl, and dream with them.

Soul Artists recognize that one of the primary languages of soul is *image*, as in
the power of imagining. Nature aside, little combines image and feeling as poetry
does—speaking to something essential, subterranean, and uncharted within us.
Something that when it rises up, offers an expanded and authentic sense of our

true self, and we realize, *yes, this is who I am.*

Ideally, we make a conscious commitment to nourishing body, mind, soul and heart each day. This is the way of the Soul Artist.

Gentle reader, even if poetry is not something that speaks to you on a heart or soul level, here's hoping that you find *something* that feels like a worthy soul practice—a conscious, deliberate action you take on a regular basis to move you closer to the very core of your authentic being—something that *nourishes* you. I wonder, what will you choose?

Knowing the entire poem now by heart, once again I borrow Ms. Oliver's eloquent and evocative words: *Tell me, what is it you plan to do with your one wild and precious life?*

*a *a *a

Death in the Garden, Beauty in Life
(September, 2014)

I knew in an instant it was dying.

As evening descended at my newly rented oceanside cottage, I was talking on the phone with my friend nearby in Carmel Valley. Gazing out at the shifting hues of sea and sky in the rocky cove, I spied a struggling band-tailed pigeon flapping and flopping across the stone terrace, and my heart lurched in a pang of dismay.

"Oh no! There's a wounded pigeon here."

I watched it career almost drunkenly into the masonry wall of a flower bed, then stumble across the gravel towards one of the Monterey cypress trees, both wings flailing irregularly.

"Oh dear," I reported softly to my friend, "it's not going to survive."

My friend C. has a fierce, untamed heart that cares deeply for all wild beings. "Send out a message to the coyotes," she suggested, "maybe they'll come down and finish it off." Her words were meant in all kindness and humanity.

I watched the bird a minute longer, sadness constricting in my chest for what I imagined to be its pain and suffering. Then I turned from the cottage windows and my conversation with C. veered off to the local coyotes—those shaggy denizens we sometimes hear in the valley *yip yipping* at the moon but who tend to stay further up in the hills.

Talking about wild ones, I relayed a freshly acquired story from BG, my new landlady, of the bobcat who came and gave birth to kittens in a sheltered corner of her property. And the mountain lion who, some years ago, ate the neighbor's cat. Contentedly fed, it lay down just outside the house to sleep until the morning, when the neighbor phoned BG in hysterics—not only that her dear little cat had been devoured but the cougar was still sleeping outside (it ran off shortly thereafter, just as BG arrived after phoning the Point Lobos ranger station).

In the refuge of the charming old poet's cottage, I hoped that some carnivorous creature would come along in the darkness and finish off the pigeon so that it didn't suffer long, but I suspected the feathered one would not make it through the night regardless.

The next morning, after greeting the dawn in my usual barefoot ritual, and some hours of writing by the window, I stepped out into the swirling, salty air and walked toward the edge of the property where it abuts the south cove. I had forgotten the winged one until I encountered it against a grey stone bordering the path, as if sleeping, its obsidian eyes open and a single black fly walking down the feathered back. *Oh dear.*

I debated briefly whether to toss it into some bushes and let one of those earlier-hoped-for feral four-leggeds eventually find it as an aged and pungent meal. Or simply hurl it over the cliff into the cove for a sea burial. Somehow, putting the bird in the rubbish bin seemed far too crass. Instead, I decided to bury it, to return this soft feathered one to dark earth—a realm that the little being of treetops and clouds knew only through its yellow taloned feet.

I walked back up the garden paths toward the cottage and BG's stone tower, looking for a suitable place to bury the forest pigeon. Near an old wooden fence and a lanky camellia bush, a towering Monterey cypress overhead, using bare hands and a flat stone I dug a suitable hole in the rich soil—a well-aged compost of dirt and cypress bits.

Returning to the lower path where the bird lay, I crouched down and gathered it in my hands. Suddenly, my heart cracked open and I wept. Walking slowly along the stone path, I spoke to the feathered body as I carried it. There were no obvious wounds, and the bright yellow feet were tucked up demurely. In my gentle grip, I could feel that beneath the soft cape of feathers, flesh and bones were already rigid.

I admired its appealing colors—breast plumage of dusky violet, a semicircle white collar at the rear of its neck, an iridescent sheen of greenish gold at the rear of its shoulders, and dark grey wings. A beautiful bird. I mourned aloud that it would no longer appreciate the beauty of this earth, sky, and sea. For despite the long hours of looking for food, and cold nights spent in the shelter of a windswept tree, surely to a forest bird's eye the world can only be beautiful. No more would this one know the pleasure of daily flight, feeding, breeding, nesting, or looking out at the ocean's frothy waves. No more days to greet at dawn, a small cooing voice silenced from the song of the world.

My belief is when the spirit of an animal winks out, another winks in, and there is no pressing reason to become overly sentimental about death. Finding a dead toad or rigid brown rat on the path would probably not have evoked such a note of sadness. The unexpected tears flowed mainly from my affection for birds, my happiness in feeding and watching them; the feathered acrobats of flight have provided countless hours of genuine delight with their twittering antics, birdspeak, and songs. The creature's stilled beauty touched me.

I so deeply love the *exquisiteness* of this world. And I held a poignant, feathered reminder in my hands that the day will come when my own heart goes silent and still. How keenly I appreciate the forms of nature, from a single flower blooming exuberantly in the garden to the wild expanse of sensual, untamed wilderness. As a Soul Artist, I am a celebrant of natural beauty, and I search it out and sing (or write) its praise. Daily. Everywhere.

Beloved, I whisper softly—to gnarled tree, jagged stone, twinkling blue stars, purring cat, twittering little bird, tanged vine, or my dear mate sleeping quietly beside me—*you are beautiful*.

What grace to be ensconced in a human body—with all its aches, pains, wobbles, wounds, grumblings, odiferous scents, frustrating limitations, and persistent hungers—walking through this world with heart and senses wide open to the symphony that surrounds. Many times I've written in these journal posts that appreciating beauty and nature's wild creation is a *soul practice*. And each of us is the Universe experiencing the imagination and creative grandeur of itself, both in shadows and light.

I crouched down and placed the soft but stiff, pretty bird into its freshly dug grave. As a warm tear fell from my eye, I wished the feathered one good dreaming and happy flying in other realms... on to the next life. Then I covered it with handfuls of fragrant, mulchy soil and laid a flat, triangular granite stone over the small grave. Perhaps doing so would discourage any four-leggeds who might sniff the body out in the days ahead and dig it up. Probably not, and it wouldn't really matter anyway.

For a moment I tarried, knees groaning in the continued squat but my heart open like wings—wide enough to embrace the world. The tenderness and appreciation I feel for my human beloved suddenly swelled, along with my dear little doglets so far away in Hawaii. Brushing soil from my hands, the silent expansion of gratitude in my chest rolled out like a wave, meeting each thing in the garden with a simple blessing.

Holy... holy.

"Doesn't everything die at last, and too soon?" enquires Mary Oliver, the Pulitzer prize–winning American poet. Indeed, how quickly death brings the preciousness of life into crystal clarity.

Ascending the steps to the top of the property and then descending to the poet's cottage, I felt both bemused and appreciative of my sentimentality for a simple bird's passing. This was only a forest dwelling, band-tailed pigeon with whom I had no recognizable relationship. All of us are only passing through, I know. Yet to be *fully human* on the journey, we suffer the beauty like an ache in our bones, appreciating these fleeing moments as they arrive, winging softly with incalculable speed and grace.

Meanwhile, life goes on. (Also a line, I just realized, in another of Mary Oliver's poems I carry in my heart.)

I did not linger in sadness as if I had lost someone dear, but my heart was wedged open a bit wider than usual as I moved through the ensuing hours. My friend C. arrived for a visit, her first time to this retreat by the sea, and we sat outside at a mosaic-tiled, rusting bistro table; observing aquamarine waves orchestrate the floating kelp, and watching sea kayakers navigate the far edges of the cove. I told her of the bird's burial, my tenderhearted sentimentality for nature, and we both quietly drank in the beauty of our surrounding world on a sunny day. Cups of quickly cooling but fine tea and something sweet to eat, listening to birdsong amid the New World cypresses and a timeless chant of the Pacific.

So often in these posts, I've offered that Soul Artists take the time to appreciate beauty. We experience life with senses ajar, engaged in a polysensory communion with the 'other-than-human' world around us. We are seduced by Eros, nature, and the Wild Beloved in ways that make us pause, a heart full of gratitude. And wonder. In such moments of unspoken *common-union*, body and soul resonate in their true, authentic directive. We grow... and shine.

Gentle reader, here's hoping you find moments to pause and appreciate what is around you. Maybe you'll join me in becoming a conscious celebrant of the overwhelming beauty that enfolds us on this journey—the ordinary sacred. We inhabit a fully participatory and reciprocating universe, in which whatever you acknowledge as beautiful is really just your own beauty, mirrored back to you.

❧ ❧ ❧

Tastes of Spring: A Trip to Farmers Market
(March, 2015)

The enticing aroma of ripe, fresh strawberries scents the air.

On a bright spring morning, I have walked from my rented cottage in Carmel-by-the-Sea to the weekly farmer's market. The assemblage of vendors is a modest affair, perhaps a dozen tables, the gathering significantly smaller now that the City exiled it from the Sunset Center parking lot. Briefly the market settled at the little park between Ocean Avenue and 6th Street, but then it was bumped from the grass to sit street-side, between Mission and Junipero where I find it today.

The morning sky aches with a song of clear blue on a day that shimmers with warmth. As with yesterday, the temperature will reach 75 Fahrenheit (23 Celsius), and having recently been in the frozen Rocky Mountain states where spring is still months away, I'm very appreciative of California's temperate climate (if still praying fervently for rain). The equinox has only just passed, but here on the central coast a colorful riot of spring is bursting forth in foliage, flowers, fruit, and vegetables. Blessed be.

Walking sandals strapped on my feet, a favorite wide-brimmed hat somewhat hiding my unruly and unbrushed hair, and toting my Provençal market basket with its leather handles, I amble unhurriedly toward the town center, utterly content to be out and about on such a gorgeous day. Moods of weather shift quickly here on the Cypress Coast, and it's possible that by lunchtime or later this afternoon the entire landscape may be draped in fog, tall trees transformed to ghostly sentinels in the trailing mists. We shall see what unfolds.

For half a dozen reasons, I have reluctantly relocated my writing retreat into town. I'm still deeply missing that dear, magical poet's cottage on the rocky cove, with sea otters to delight me, and the rumbling waves a constant presence. Almost every day when I am here, I walk the few blocks to the shops or a bit further to the long, white sandy beach. Part of such an outing is for the exercise, to move my *bodysoul* and escape from the confines of a tiny, down-at-heel house where I spend much of my day quietly holed up, stringing words into sentences like glittering beads on a necklace. But there is also the simple delight of strolling through the environs of this charming little village set among coastal pines and elegant Monterey cypresses. And if you read this column at all regularly, you know I am big on small, everyday delights.

There are no residential sidewalks, so I ramble quietly through tree-lined streets, admiring quaint cottages and gardens clustered closely together, each one different (and costing a fortune). Every time I go walking, intuitively I choose a different route, following a zigzagging path with senses cast ajar, stopping frequently to admire whatever catches my eye—some adorable casita or *petite maison*, an alluring garden, a brightly flowering bush, a particularly stately or picturesque tree, or any of the amusing denizens that I share this place with—Crow, Jay, and Squirrel, to name a few of the noisier ones. Bless them all.

The market has just opened for the morning when I arrive. In my usual way, I walk through once just to scan quickly what is here and available, even if I mostly know what's on offer from the previous week. Regularly, there is a new discovery with things coming into season, the first of a crop, especially in spring and summer. Having scouted briefly, I circle back to make another pass, this time looking more closely and taking time at each of the vendor stalls that interest me. Whose produce looks best? It doesn't take long at a market this small—unlike larger ones that I have come to know and love in my journeys, like the *marchés* in France, and my perennial favorite in Santa Fe, New Mexico, my former haunt. I bypass anything grown conventionally, focusing only on what is *organic*, which narrows the choices further, though here in California what meets my criteria is a far greater selection than in Hawaii (where I officially live right now). Less costly, too.

The short, Mexican farmer with a sun-weathered face, wearing a red plaid cotton shirt and bushy dark mustache, sees me eyeing his piled jumble of small, multi-hued potatoes, and offers me a plastic bag. His eyebrows raise when I answer in Spanish, telling him that I already have several bags in my basket. "Hablas español," he smiles approvingly, the comment somewhere between an observation and a question. His surprise heightens when, continuing in Spanish, I share that I used to live in Spain, in Andalucía amid the olive groves. Disappointingly, his pretty potatoes aren't organic but conventional, so I don't buy any (I'm not keen on potatoes, regardless) but I wish him a good day and tip my hat.

Strawberries are the star of the morning, their scent tempting everyone who passes. Decidedly, these overly large Californian varietals aren't the sweetest or most flavorful; they were bred for sturdiness and to survive long transport distances. Wistfully, I muse for a moment, recalling the small red jewels of Oregon and France, strawberries as tender, sweet and juicy as a lover's warm kiss on your tongue. They don't last but a day at their peak, and cannot possibly be shipped across a state or country, which makes them all the more precious and wonderful. They embody *local* at its delicious, mouthwatering best. Alas, the super-sized Californians will have to do, and I will gratefully savor them for their own merit, an opening prelude to spring.

Early blackberries are arriving and, though not here yet, soon the glorious fresh peas will appear (rhapsodized over in a post from late last spring, "A Bowl of Peas"). I can hardly wait.

From the plump, soft-spoken hispanic girl with shy but flashing dark eyes, I buy short nubby carrots with pale golden skin, a sizable bushel of fragrant cilantro ("fresh coriander" my UK friends call it), a vibrant bunch of rainbow chard (I can never resist the assortment of multicolored stalks) with glistening dark leaves, and some tender broccoli rabe. All so fresh and crisp that it seems to hum quietly in my hands.

At the next table, I purchase a dozen eggs in an assortment of colors from the Free Range Egg Lady, as her sign says. Her orange permanent mascara eyebrows look abnormally bright behind oversize eyeglasses, but they match the curly locks of copper orange hair winging loose and rowdy from beneath her blue baseball cap. The eggs are beautiful and I long to place them in an attractive basket on the counter as I did in Europe—where eggs, even after being washed, are never sold refrigerated—to admire the collection of pastel hues. (In the States, we're told that once eggs have been refrigerated, they should remain that way, but I suspect that is simply the paranoia of neo-Pasteurians in an age fearfully obsessed with bacteria.)

I pause at the table of apples and fresh-pressed juices, debating for a minute, my eyes sweeping the selection. These must be fruit held in cold storage, given their growing season has long passed, but how I relish a nice Pink Lady—crisp and sweet with a slightly tart edge. Likely these will disappoint, and I can almost hear my dear, spooky friend Sara (whose business is growing organic apples in Kent, England) telling me to pass, but I plunk three into the trusty basket. I figure if they turn out to be too lackluster for eating on their own, these Pinks can always be blitzed up in the Vitamix as part of my daily green smoothie.

It seems enough. I'm on my own for the next two weeks, working away on Book 2 (my England memoir), and solo meals at the cottage are usually modest. Mostly vegetables and salads, with an occasional bit of wild-caught fish or organic poultry to keep things interesting. On market day, I like to have the fridge empty so that lunch and supper can be as fresh as possible (ever lacking a vegetable garden in my nomadic life). Sometimes, however, as today, I find myself still needing to use up a few items previously purchased. There's the last of the pencil-thin asparagus I bought. And the local globe artichoke I am envisioning with a bowl of pungent, Provençal *aïoli* made with unctuous olive oil and garlic cloves pounded in a mortar and pestle. (I'm alone and can gorge contentedly on said garlicky sauce without offending my mate or having to sleep in a different room. Bring it on, I say.)

In multiple SAJ posts over the past years (you can find them under Slow Food in the archives), I have written of my delight in farmers' markets; my gratitude for the fresh bounty they offer, my sincere appreciation for such hardworking people, and how happy I am to press money into the well-calloused hands that grew the food I consume. I've said it repeatedly: it matters what we eat, how it was raised and produced, and where we purchased it. Not simply for our own health, wellbeing, and sense of soul, but as a species in our relationship to this planet where we are an integral (and hugely influential) component.

Returning to the cottage beneath a still enduring blue sky, there is a happy hum in my core. The opportunity to put a face and smile with otherwise anonymous food, to inch closer to sustainability, and to be deeply nourished—literally—by sustenance grown locally in a way that honors and nurtures the earth, it all feeds my soul. The French market basket is gently weighted with gorgeous produce and fragrant strawberries, and I am enfolded by a brilliantly warm spring day as my mind considers what I will cook later. All the while, I'm simultaneously enjoying the trees, cottages, gardens, and birds of this coastal neighborhood.

If there is a theme that weaves continually through these posts, it's exploring the ways we nourish the soul through the simple celebrations of being human—those everyday moments where the ordinary intersects the sacred and we realize that, ultimately, little difference exists between the two. Walking to market on a fine morning is one such event that can so easily be a celebration. When our senses and heart are open and we're paying attention, that is.

Soul Artists know the daily moments and events of life are the warp and weft of the richly woven tapestry of our existence. Some threads are thicker, darker, or coarser, while others shimmer brightly as if spun from pure gold. With a bit of perspective, we see that these experiences form patterns, familiar shapes, and passages of our lives. Meanwhile, the weaving goes on. Another day, another dozen—or a hundred—different threads interwoven with the mundane tasks and pleasures of being embodied as a sensual soul in a vast garden of small wonders... like fresh strawberries in a pretty bowl, perfuming the kitchen, waiting to be savored.

Gentle reader, here's hoping that something in your day feels like a simple celebration. Dinner placed on the table, fragrant and enticing. Pulling weeds in the garden, or planting fresh seeds beneath a gentle covering of dirt. A walk through the neighborhood, admiring what's in bloom and listening to birdsong. Curling up with your beloved, feeling their heartbeat and breath. A new poem read aloud by candlelight, or spilling forth from a favorite pen onto paper. The visceral power of the body freed by a great shout or roar. A trip to farmer's market to appreciate and gather what is local and fresh from the good earth.

Here in the Northern Hemisphere, spring bulbs dreaming of sunshine and color push eagerly forth from dark soil, bursting with new life. Every moment is a gift if we can choose to see it as such, and I wonder what you will most deeply appreciate today.

If I could deliver you a perfect ripe, enticingly fragrant strawberry, I would.

❧ ❧ ❧

Qigong and the Blue Jay

(June, 2016)

In a thrum of wings, a Western scrub jay alighted atop the tall, wooden front gate.

"Hello, lovely," I smiled, pausing my Qigong practice, barefoot on the cool red bricks. For a moment he perched there, observing, scanning for the Whippets, then flew just over my head with a quick cadence of wingbeats—so low that the wind of his passing ruffled my hair—and landed on the bird feeder, newly relocated to the center of the front garden.

I resumed my breath and coordinated movements for the Lung Meridian, grinning as he balanced on the feeder's post, not three feet away, rummaging with a glossy beak through the bird food for his preferred sunflower seeds, tossing the less desirable options aside and over the edge.

I know this blue-winged fellow. I've been feeding him for over a year and call him Jasper, regardless that it may very well be a female. Before the Sussex Duo arrived from the islands (part of the transition to a full-time, mainland existence), and prior to having the bird feeder, he would come within arm's reach at the wooden railing where I scattered the birdseed. Or right to the small bistro table on the deck where I sit to write and eat lunch on sunny days. In the mornings, if breakfast wasn't served by a reasonable hour, I would hear him outside, screeching noisily in the tree, calling to me. Cheeky chap.

Regrettably, Pippin in particular likes to chase away any bird that alights on the deck, even sometimes at the feeder, which has diminished my garden visitors somewhat. Except the squirrels, who are undeterred and willing to risk life and limb to gobble up the fallen seeds, and delight in tormenting the dogs, I suspect. Jasper is braver than the little dark-eyed Oregon juncos that visit, and he's even bolder than Patch the Crow (so-named for a ruffled, whitish flaw in his breast feathers).

The Sussex Duo were in the house taking another nap and I was outside, doing my Qigong barefoot on the earth, recovering from too much time spent on the computer. This past week, I have spent countless hours building a new website, and despite breaks to go outdoors for *earthing*, the considerable project has pushed the limits of what I can handle as I struggle with electromagnetic hypersensitivity

(EHS).

Being barefoot on the earth and doing my daily Qigong is restorative, indeed; a counterpose to the so-called "virtual" wired work. Irrespective that it is June, the weather here on the central California coast remains cool and cloudy with a marine layer of fog (the infamous "June gloom"), and my exposed feet and hands felt slightly chilled.

Every day, I am dreaming of summer and hoping it will finally arrive but still it remains elusive. August, perhaps...?

Progressing through the sequence of exercises for the meridians (invisible, subtle channels of magnetic energy that traditional Chinese Medicine discovered eons ago), I pushed away the distractions and noises. My crazy neighbor on the north side was out front of her house, working on one of the endless projects in her scrapyard, talking loudly to herself—arguing, apparently with her invisible guides, or just a very fractured self. On the southerly side of my cottage, the neighbor's gardener employed his noisy leaf blower, one of my *least* favorite modern noisemakers. Just across the street, a house is being demolished to build a new one, so I am living in a daily deconstruction zone.

The external environment seemed anything but tranquil, and my internal world rumbled with its own share of distractions. I buzzed with slight angst that I'd not yet written the SAJ post to go out early the next morning (Sunday, as always), wondering what I would write about this week. And I still rattled with the latest disappointments in my quest to get the England memoir published.

In the current search for a literary agent and the rejections that come along with that, with each one who has declined (or simply ignored) my query letter, I have silently said *thank you;* realizing they are not the right person to represent my work.

"The perfect person will be interested," I said aloud, refocusing upon breath and movements. Simultaneously, I admired the fading yellow rose nearby, the lacy limbs of the Grandmother Monterey cypress above me swaying in a coastal breeze, and the vintage red bricks beneath my bare soles.

This moment, here and now, is nothing but the ordinary sacred, I reminded myself.

May I inhabit it fully, noise and all, both internal and external, with unclad feet on the ground, seeking *balance*.

And I could not help but be cheered by the company of Jasper the Jay, who wasn't the least perturbed by the morning's mental angst, nor my sweeping arm gestures for the Kidney/Bladder Meridian. He kept a glassy eye turned toward me, watching my odd behavior and movements.

"Are you the blue bird of happiness?" I asked.

Of course I am, his return glance said wordlessly, *I was wondering when you would finally clue in.*

He/she is a beautiful bird, I think. Vivid blue wings, crest and tail, and a grey underbelly and back patch, with a grey racing stripe just over the black "cheeks." Recently, a dear friend visited from England, where Western scrub jays are unknown, and as Jasper perched at the feeder, she remarked on his/her attractiveness. It warms my heart, this modest connection with a few denizens of this place, and as I've written elsewhere, feeding the birds and little wild ones is what any Green Man—that Old World archetype of the Sacred Masculine— would do.

In *The Bones and Breath*, I've offered that the heart of sacred masculinity rests in the appreciation of nature and wild beauty, honoring our interconnectedness, and the appropriate use of personal power, all while embracing empathy and compassion. Love, really. Surely we could say the same of the Divine Feminine. Together they represent balance and wholeness within each of us as well as the larger story.

Balance. Sometimes it seems elusive to me as blue sky here on the coast. Yet with "unplugging" from work and technology, stepping outdoors for Qigong and reconnecting to a larger story—if only a segment of the day in this front garden while the marine layer rolls in—I endeavor to find it. Even briefly. Knowing I'll lose it again but somehow it's all part of this curious journey.

Meanwhile, Jasper balances effortlessly on the bird feeder, gobbling up sunflower seeds.

You humans make everything too complicated, he casts me a knowing look. *It's really quite simple. Expectation and disappointment always trip you up.*

So true. What a wise little Master... cleverly disguised as a cheeky, blue and grey bird.

Gentle reader, I wish you the grace of *balance* in your day—even briefly. Equilibrium between work and play, between a wired and technological existence versus a more natural, healthy and old-fashioned one, between domesticity and soulful wildness. May you reconcile the aspects of yourself and life so often at odds. Or simply *rest*. It seems to me the elusive balancing point is just an ongoing process of relinquishing our own agendas and attachments, surrendering to disappointment and moving on, still bravely following the truth of one's heart and soul.

Myself, I'm trying to see the perfection in it all, imperfect as it seems.

Barefoot on the earth. Befriending the blue bird of happiness.

🐦 🐦 🐦

Washing the Dishes, Tending the Earth

(August, 2015)

I'm washing dishes in a white plastic tub in the kitchen sink.

Admittedly, I am not keen on plastic, in general. Never mind that it lingers around to junk up the planet forever, the aesthete in me simply finds it cheap and unappealing. I prefer things that are handmade, elemental, and have some semblance of character or charm. *Soul*, even. Petroleum-based products don't warm my heart, and I've long since banished plastic from my house wherever I can. So it's a bit out of character that a flimsy, generic tub sits in my sink day after day.

California is entering its fourth consecutive year of drought, the worst in recorded history. To reduce personal water use, along with brief showers, not letting the faucet run when I brush my teeth or shave, and only flushing the toilet when necessary, I decided that another simple action I can take is washing dishes in a tub and then pouring the "grey water" onto the deck and garden plants outdoors. (Earth-friendly, biodegradable dish soap required, of course.)

Standing at the sink while rinsing my favorite, handmade ceramic tea cup, I recall many years ago reading *The Miracle of Mindfulness*, by Thich Naht Hahn, celebrated Vietnamese monk and teacher. That was the first time I encountered his famous teaching of "washing the dishes to wash the dishes," an everyday practice in being *present* and mindful. Often when alone, I find myself in a quiet meditation with hands, sponge, warm sudsy water, cutlery and crockery. Breathing in, breathing out. Belly soft. Shoulders relaxed.

Taking things one step further, washing the dishes could become a simple gesture of conscious relationship with place—being mindful not only of the actual process of *washing* but also the water being used. Certainly, I can use less of a precious resource and then recycle it among the plants with whom I share this thirsty patch of earth.

Imagine if just one person in twenty—or a hundred—washed their dishes modestly in a tub and recycled the water. California could conserve uncountable millions of gallons.

Years ago, my partner and I bought a rustic but charming house on the lush, windward side of the Big Island of Hawaii, where our water supply came from a large concrete catchment tank. It was open at the top (covered with nylon mesh) to catch the rain, and the gutters along the roof eaves drained into it as well. From the tank into the house, the water went through a multistage filtering system. Normally, precipitation was abundant (it was a rainforest, after all) but during occasional dry periods the catchment's level dropped low, and we learned to always be prudent.

One day while visiting the mainland, sipping green tea with a friend, I shared about our eco-friendly catchment system. She set down her cup with a perplexed look.

"What do you mean your water comes from rain?"

I explained it again: precipitation, tank, filter. She was dumbfounded. Confused. Slightly repulsed.

"Just where do you think your water comes from?" I enquired with a wry smile.

"Well, from the faucet."

Right. She had honestly never considered the water supply beyond that. The fact that this life-sustaining element flows directly into our homes, clean and more or less ready to drink (I prefer mine filtered, thank you), is a minor miracle that most people simply take for granted. Never mind where it comes from or goes. Not unlike our overly wasteful packaging and rubbish, all carted away somewhere pleasantly out of sight and mind, but steadily filling up the landfills and littering our environment.

Little is more insidious than the thought, *my actions as an individual don't matter in the larger scheme.* Nothing could be further from the truth. The way that change comes to the world is seldom from the top and down, but through a slowly building wave of countless, small actions.

Wendell Berry—acclaimed essayist, novelist, poet, and gentle activist who has consciously farmed a hillside in Kentucky for more than four decades—wrote in his brilliant collection of essays, *Bringing It to the Table: On Farming and Food*, that eating is an "agricultural act." Berry was an early and eloquent voice proclaiming what we eat matters, not only in reforming America's food system but also in our intimate relationship with place and each other.

If you read these posts at all regularly, likely you're already familiar with my conviction that what we eat and how we live matters. Our choices bear consequence not only to our own health, well-being, and sense of soul, but also as a species to this planet of which we are an integral (and disproportionately influential) part.

So too with washing the dishes.

More than just *mindful,* responsible, or even political, doing the "washing up" in an unappealing plastic tub is a quiet gesture of conscious relationship with the place I dwell. An opportunity to step outside and feel the earth beneath my bare feet—sole and soul meeting soil—and deliver very welcome hydration to the blooming pink camellias, some pots of fragrant herbs and lavender, a spindly rose bush, the lone cherry tree. An action that says, *you matter and I appreciate you.*

Despite our anthropocentric arrogance, it is largely the plants, mycelium, and microbes that make our life on earth even possible. Other beings have a right to be here as much as we do, and one may discover a gentle, soul nurturing grace in communion with them. As I repeatedly offer in this column and in my book, *The Bones and Breath: A Man's Guide to Eros, the Sacred Masculine, and the Wild Soul,* "*everything* is relationship."

In America, washing dishes is not a common path to the holy. Yet if hearts widen and senses open to the living web that surrounds, when we are present in body and breath, even a simple action resonates with power of the sacred. I say a tub of dishwater is not too humble to offer to the Soul of the World.

With some grace and mindfulness, may we all be fed, watered, and nourished deeply down to our interconnected roots.

❧ ❧ ❧

The Decorator Rat

(May, 2015)

I almost regret killing him.

Who would have guessed he possessed such an eye for home decorating?

I'm referring to the rat that shared our house for almost a month at the year-end holidays, keeping us awake at night and eluding all manner of traps and poison until, thanks to some peanut butter, it finally met its end in the electric Rat Zapper (delivers an electric shock sufficient to kill a large rodent). Gruesome, I know, but swift.

I admit that killing our four-legged, furry visitor was less-than-Buddhist. Certainly, it did not move me closer to embodying kinship with all life. Yet rats in Hawaii carry typhus, leptospirosis, bubonic plague, and a host of other nasties; for health safety reasons alone, I simply couldn't share the kitchen counters with him or her.

Three different kinds of rats reside in these islands: roof (or tree) rats; Norway wharf rats; and Polynesian field rats (the only ones that surf). I suspected our visitor was a roof rat because he/she was smaller, and kept escaping up to the loft; more than once, I'd seen it deftly climbing up and down the kitchen cabinets en route. I ascertained the house entry and exit point was one of the ceiling beams, and we could hear him climbing inside the wall of our bedroom. Yet the trap I placed upstairs remained empty.

Then, a couple of weeks ago, I entered the kitchen one morning and noted the red blinking light on the recently acquired Zapper, indicating a dead rat inside. Sure enough, a slender and hairless tail protruded motionless from the contraption. I took the black plastic rectangular device outside to the trees at the edge of the property, away from where our English Whippets would find it, and squatted down. Tilting the electrocution box in my hands, I watched a brown rat slide out onto the carpet of dried leaves. Looking at the motionless, limp creature, I felt a bit sad (and fully responsible) for its death. A dark glass eye stared lifelessly at me while I admired the soft, mottled fur on its body. I'm no expert but, as far as rats go, it was an attractive one, I say.

I walked back inside, washed my hands, and carried on with the morning. *Sans rat. Enfin.*

As I wrote in last week's post ["Spirits of Cedar: A Walk on the Mountain"], Maui has been rocked by intense storms. The heavily patched, somewhat dodgy, forty year-old roof of this rented cottage began to leak impressively in the heavy monsoon rains. Oh joy. Our small, shared office is accessed by a carpeted ladder, and as I considered the massive amount of water pouring down outside, I noticed the large, triangular skylight in the loft was leaking again. Climbing up, I found the printer resting in a puddle of water on its wooden chest, the recycling basket holding a soup of wet paper and bleeding ink, and the sloped, wooden ceiling was hemorrhaging along new seams. Boxes and luggage stashed under the incline were getting soaked, so I began pulling them forward in hopes that I could prevent further damage to our goods. I would place buckets under the leaking areas and, in the meantime, pray the entire house wouldn't wash down the slopes of Haleakalā in a muddy torrent coursing over the front steps and still rising.

In the process of shuffling boxes and luggage, I noted a fair amount of rat droppings and chewed debris. Indeed, the more boxes I moved the more evidence I discovered our furry friend had been up here for quite a while... nesting and pooping.

As I maneuvered an antique, small chest of drawers to gain access to soggy boxes behind, a black mesh bag caught my eye. I paused, staring at the item on the floor while my brain struggled for a minute to make the connection. What was it doing there? Normally it holds my "solar shower" (a handy contraption with a large water bladder and attached hose with nozzle, that I take on camping and backpacking trips; simply fill it with water and place it in the sun, and in a short while you have warm, even hot, water). I had taken the kit out a couple of weeks earlier to use as a hot water bottle and, a few days later when I went to put it away, couldn't locate the black mesh bag. This utterly puzzled me. I'm a very tidy, organized person – not the sort to casually misplace something or put it away in the wrong spot. Baffled, I looked around for the bag, even in places where I knew it couldn't possibly be, and in the end, unable to find it, simply placed the solar shower back in my large plastic bin of camping gear. Very odd, indeed.

Over the past month or two, other things have gone missing in the loft, similarly leaving me perplexed. A couple of them I attributed immediately to Mr. Rat, including a small nylon gift bag of Anasazi beans, a packet of wildflower seeds, and a ziplock sandwich bag containing heirloom blue corn. All were tokens from a dear mentor's beautiful, remarkable and inspiring wedding as chronicled in my post, "A Soul Artist Wedding" (as well as the Riverspeak podcast episode, "A Feast of Love"). These items had vanished from the ornately carved Balinese altar that holds my special objects, and when I noticed their disappearance, I lamented the rat must have eaten them. A small beeswax candle from England had also gone missing from the altar, and this too I blamed on our hungry, noisy visitor (albeit surprised that he/she had a taste for beeswax). Either he was entirely undiscerning in his tastes or highly gourmet. Cheeky little bastard.

Most baffling, however, was the disappearance of a blue, silken drawstring bag embroidered with silver dolphins that enclosed a deck of divination cards called The Shaman's Oracle (in case you are curious). At the holidays, a guest from Oahu had slept on the floor of the loft; in preparation, I rearranged things a bit to make room for the camping pad, and tucked the oracle cards in their satin bag behind a decorative pillow on a wooden chair. After our friend's departure, tidying the loft, I retrieved the cards from where I had stashed them and discovered the bag was missing. Again, how odd. I thought it highly unlikely that J. would have stolen it (he's not that sort of fellow), but I felt deeply puzzled. I decided not to mention it to my partner.

Staring down at the formerly missing mesh bag visible beneath the old chest, the pieces finally clicked. The rat had dragged it there, but... why? Reaching to draw out the black sack, I saw a two-inch clearance under the back of the furniture piece. What a cozy, protected spot for a rat nest.

Moving a heavy, wet box of files to have some room, I knelt down to peer cautiously underneath the oak dresser, hoping I would not be suddenly surprised by the emergence of another rat. Rodents are seldom solitary creatures; the fact I had killed one didn't mean there weren't more.

I craned my neck and peeked warily underneath... and almost laughed aloud in surprise.

No rat, just a well decorated little nest of missing items (and a copious amount of small, dark turds).

I stood, grabbed ahold of the dresser sides and maneuvered the solid piece towards the center of the loft. In the revealed space, framed by flattened indentions in the carpet from the dresser, were the following:

- The miniature, burgundy gift bag of Anasazi beans from Annie's wedding, still tied with its ribbon (beans intact)
- The packet of wildflower seeds that marked each wedding guest's place at respective tables (thoroughly chewed and seeds eaten)
- Shredded remains of the ziplock plastic sandwich bag that previously held a handful of heirloom blue corn (eaten)
- The small, golden beeswax taper from my altar (unchewed and intact)
- The embroidered blue satin drawstring bag missing from the The Shaman's Oracle
- Four, floatable rubber ducks, each one outfitted for Christmas, a gift from my friend in the UK who collects such dapper little "quackers"

I crouched down, rocking on my heels, and marveled at the rat's collection. What a cache. Who would have guessed...?

Carefully I lifted the satin bag and examined it, appreciating that it was not chewed or damaged in any way. I guess he/she simply fancied the pretty satchel and wanted it for home decor. Mind you, the bag had been cinched snugly around the cards. Thus, the rat had to first discover the cards on the chair (stashed behind the decorative pillow), work the cloth bag open and pull it off the deck, and then drag it back to its nest on the far side of the loft while our guest slept – dreaming to the sounds of scurrying little feet. Most impressive. (J. will never sleep at our house again after reading this, I'm certain.)

I picked up each of the Christmas ducks, noting that one had been slightly chewed on its bright yellow bum but no other damage. The floatable rubber toys had been inside a large, copper bowl used for an Ayurvedic treatment called *shirodhara* (a thin stream of warm sesame oil poured continuously upon the forehead; a deeply relaxing treatment that calms the nervous system and pacifies Vata *dosha*), on the opposite side of the loft from the oak chest. Each duck had been removed from the bowl and carried to the sanctuary under the dresser. Four ducks, four trips. Quite the haul. I took them downstairs to wash and disinfect them in the sink (alas, the little dude with a hole in his arse no longer floats quite so well).

Over the years, friends have gifted me a handful of truly remarkable tales regarding their notable interactions with various wild animals. While I'm not sure our Hawaiian decorator rat earns a place in the same league as those special stories, I can't help but muse on his/her unusual nest. Something touched me in its discovery, and I feel a renewed appreciation for smaller, four-legged lives.

Despite humanity's self-importance as the perceived apex of creation, really, we are only one part of the web. I suppose it is for each of us to ask, *what are the ways we might share, and with whom?*

Surely, he/she felt this was their house as much as I feel it is mine (albeit rented). And certainly, we all deserve a sanctuary and cozy nest, a haven from the trials and troubles of the world – a well-decorated one, at that. Little rat, *e kala mai* ("I'm sorry" in Hawaiian). I salute your style. And I will remember you in future holiday seasons when those dapper Christmas ducks come out.

Meet the Green Man:
Archetype for A Wild Soul

(August, 2015)

After days of cold, grey rain dampening my spirit, I needed to get out and walk. Move my bones. Enliven my soul. Yes, indeed, and thank the gods for sun.

Opening the gate in the tall deer fence, I stepped through into the soggy field with its newly sprouted carpet of vividly green English wheat. The sky shimmered blue and a sheer, golden light illuminated the bare trees and the rolling South Downs in the distance.

Full of gratitude for the clear day, I headed south from our West Sussex cottage at the edge of a vast estate and working farm, my rubber Wellies squashing noisily through waterlogged grass and mud at the edge of the field. I had no clear intention of where I would walk but wished to avoid any roads, keeping only soft, wet earth underfoot, and thus wandered footpaths that wove like bedraggled ribbons over wooded hill and dale.

Tromping along a muddy track, relishing both my exercise and being enfolded by trees and fields, I found myself reflecting on the Green Man, an ancient pagan archetype of masculine connection with nature.

Far older than Christianity, the Green Man reemerged powerfully in the twelfth century, and his image can be found carved into stone pillars in churches throughout Europe. At the sacred site of Chartres, France, he appears at least seventy-two times within the great cathedral, and over a hundred of his stone faces decorate Rosslyn Chapel in Scotland.

Depicted with beard and hair growing or formed of leaves, vines, and boughs, the Green Man is the steward of forests and land. He embodies a silent, gentle wisdom through his respect of all living things and their interpenetration. Inherently masculine, the bearded visage models a different kind of manhood and strength: based on relationship, caring, and true husbandry or stewardship. In a unique and timeless way, he gives us a powerful metaphor and embodiment of the Sacred Masculine.

A mild breeze tousling my unruly hair, feeling – or perhaps wishfully imagining – the early notes of spring, I was unconsciously heading for the mossy dell where I first sensed his presence. And with a note of hopefulness, I wondered whether I would detect his nuanced energy there again.

෮෨

Residing in southern England, particularly when I wandered through whispering woods or less domesticated places, the Green Man often entered my consciousness. On some subtle level, his energy remains present in the British Isles, still existing in the wilder landscapes and surfacing as part of regional folklore.

Often called Jack of the Wood, or Jack of the Green, he is the basis for popular mythic characters such as the Green Knight in the Arthurian legend of Sir Gawain, and also Robin Hood. In his classic guise, the Green Man seems to be reemerging and growing in newfound popularity around the globe, appearing on anything from t-shirts to websites.

Yet one doesn't have to be a neo-pagan to appreciate this ancient, archetypal energy of malehood entwined with nature and mystery. We don't have to follow any religion at all. We simply need to possess a sense of *soul*.

In a recent article written for the Good Men Project, drawing a thread from *The Bones and Breath: A Man's Guide to Eros, the Sacred Masculine, and the Wild Soul*, I offered that our culture lacks authentic rites of passage, soulful initiations, and wise elders. In a materialistic society where notions of *soul* aren't really valued or supported, many of us men are searching for deeper meaning in life. In that quest, we seek a positive, affirming embodiment of the masculine connected to something larger than simply ego, personal gain, and materialism. Men need role models who teach and demonstrate we each have something essential to bring to our community and the world, mentors who understand that everything is related to everything else, and the heart is a true compass.

Looking for a such a role model or affirming embodiment of the masculine, if we turn to classic myths and archetypes we could find multiple metaphors that represent the Sacred Masculine – or at least partial aspects, if somewhat too polarized and dualistic.

Enter the Green Man: a strong and compassionate masculine who respects the hidden laws of nature and interwoven relationship. In a modern incarnation, he stands for environmental awareness and action; symbolizing cooperation with nature rather than dominion over it for resources, wealth, and power. In a sense, he is the original eco-warrior. Somehow, with his gentleness and Earth-focused nature, the Green Man seems both relevant and approachable. To me, he does.

❧

These days, I reside in the New World again, and on my walks in the wilds and semi-wilds of this continent, I don't sense the Green Man as I did in England. Yet I seem to have taken on that archetypal energy in a different manner:

He is *in* me.

He's reflected in the choices I make with food: where was it raised, how was it produced, and how far has it traveled to reach me? When I shop at the weekly farmer's market and press money directly into the hands of those who tended the earth and grew the ingredients for my supper, the Green Man is there.

He is present when I wash my dishes in a plastic tub in the sink and then pour the water onto the plants on my California deck and garden with a gentle blessing. His energy is an awareness of my carbon footprint, driving less and staying local, and having a fuel-efficient automobile.

The Green Man is awake when we endeavor to buy and use *less*, whenever we recycle and reuse as much as possible – for Nature never wastes anything. We embody this Sacred Masculine archetype when we practice stewardship and remember that *everything* is in relationship with everything else.

The ancient bearded man of the wood also represents and personifies something essential that most of us have lost: the wild soul.

Nearly everyone in modern culture is thoroughly domesticated and very disconnected from any sense of nature – irrespective that we *are* nature, right down to our microbes. Wedded to technology and distractions, any sense of *wildness* has been effectively banished from our air-conditioned lives. The result is that we are severed from a deeper, authentic sense of ourselves, from our innate power and visceral energy. (To be clear, I mean wildness as in nature and soul, not *destructive*.)

I am referring to something more than merely "Nature Deficit Disorder." Essential as our connection with nature is, the vast majority of people could benefit from some broader *re-wilding*, as I like to put it: a loosening of our suits, neckties, and familiar restrictions. A bit of dirt under the fingertips, some foraged greens on the plate. Time spent on the land in any kind of weather rather than parked at a desk in front of a computer. A reconnection with something more feral than fashionable might just do our souls a world of good.

As I've suggested in my book, the *wild soul* is the authentic, creative, timeless core within us – the part that not only connects to and appreciates nature, but also *is nature*. We evolved from it and remain a part of it. Again, right down to our intrinsic microbes.

∾

During the years in England, I spent uncountable hours contentedly roaming that green land. Beneath a heavy grey sky, crossing tidy fields bordered with hedgerows, or wandering through shady dells and copses, I met sly red foxes, white-spotted deer, and bounding rabbits, communed with gnarled oak trees, and somehow became a part of the very landscape. Senses open and ajar, I felt not only the hum of my own wild soul – expansion in my heart, a low buzz of visceral power in my body – but also a kinship with the living earth. We are not separate, after all, despite our perceptions and beliefs.

Whenever I walk in wild places – anywhere, really – and see the world not merely as an assortment of separate objects, or even an *ecosystem*, but rather an interconnected, creative relationship, that is the Green Man and the Sacred Masculine embodied.

Sometimes he looks just like me, but it is the Green Man who daily feeds the scrub jays, dark-eyed juncos, hummingbirds, and noisy crows with whom I share this patch of earth. He's there when I sit on the front porch in the cool evenings, a cashmere scarf wrapped round my neck, observing the light fade amid windswept Monterey cypresses, or watching the silver fog roll in to blanket the town. Listening for the deeper song of the world.

In his wordless affirming way, the Green Man teaches that the wild soul and the Sacred Masculine are essential parts of the whole, and that we are all interconnected – human, non-human, and planetary.

Friend, irrespective of gender, somewhere in your soul there's a wild man of the wood waiting to be discovered and embodied. May you meet him soon. The Great Work is at hand – humankind's evolution from being the single-most destructive element of the planet to becoming a life-sustaining, interconnected one instead – and as conscious beings every one of us is needed to accomplish that turning.

Standing alongside the Divine Feminine, the return of an earth-centric Sacred Masculine would be timely indeed.

❧ ❧ ❧

Of Hearth and Home: A Return

(February, 2015)

I *may have no home but how good to be here.*

So muses the man as he sweeps a carpet of cypress needles fallen on the deck and front walkway, the cornstalk broom in his hands rasping in a familiar voice as it brushes the ground rhythmically, an ever widening clean wake where it passes.

He has been away on travels, far across a cold grey sea, in northern lands where the freezing depths of winter still hold sway and darkness, like an earnest lover, arrives early and withdraws late. Traveling in the Old World always delights him, and immersed in a mélange of languages and cultures, he feels curiously at ease. Europe has been his residence more than once, and whenever he returns there is a curious sense of coming home, even as a foreigner.

Traveling abroad opens his senses. Literally. The novelty of a new locale causes the brain to dilate sensory gating channels from their habituated, narrowed state, and an expanded perspective of life floods one's being. He enjoys feeling the different energetic vibration and pulse of a new place. The world's great old cities seduce him with their arts and culture, the historic architecture alongside contemporary, the varied cuisines and intriguing diversity of people. All of it a welcome change of scene.

Yet in his heart he remains a quiet soul who moves at a slower, unhurried pace—more suited to countryside than bustling city. One who savors rambling walks in nature, a tranquil garden, and twinkling stars at night, his is a mostly old-fashioned life unplugged from television, radio, and the bulk of modern media. Trees are often his chosen companions, and silence is a comfortable space to inhabit.

Standing barefoot outdoors, wooden broomstick in hand, he relishes the tactile reconnection of sole, soul, and soil after too many hours hurtling through the atmosphere in the belly of a giant metal bird. The frenzied jostle and chaos of airports, the buzzing electromagnetic energy and noise, the queues and crowds funneling through transportation security and boarding the plane; all of it he finds tiresome, the most draining and tedious part of traveling. Now, feeling the cool of bricks underfoot, the roughness of bark fragments and sloughed-off bits of Monterey cypress on the spongy earth, he feels at ease—nervous system unwinding gently, a general slowing down, softening of belly and breath—a sense of coming home to himself via connection to earth.

Sweeping near the front gate, shepherding detritus into a pile, he listens to a scrub jay noisily gossiping in the neighbor's tree and a crow laughing gutturally in response down the street. The early February day shines unseasonably warm beneath a sky of pale Wedgwood blue, and the man halts his tidying work to roll up the long sleeves of his shirt. After a fortnight of being bundled in a heavy coat, woven hat, and cashmere scarf to protect against freezing fangs of weather any time he stepped out of the hotel, balmy sunshine is a true gift. The stark, grey and denuded world of northern European winter has vanished into memory, and the living scenario here enfolding him pulses green, fully alive, and blossoming.

On the central California coast, the signs of early spring are everywhere. Since his departure, the two small, spindly cherry trees beside the weathered wooden fence have burst into bright bloom, profusely decorated with inch-wide ruffled pink pompoms of spun silk. Tender and fleeting, already they litter the ground with delicate petals like large, rosy snowflakes. The camellia bushes with their dark, shiny leaves are heavily studded with scores of straining but tightly closed globes, each one a concentration of energy and colour, nearly ready to dramatically unfurl into flowered beauty. A fat American robin pecks intently at the earth, digging for breakfast, while overhead in the boughs of a venerable Monterey cypress, two red squirrels chase each other madly and noisily through the twisted maze of branches in an early spring mating chase. All of it feels welcome. Nurturing and good.

The front of the cottage swept and tidied, the man scatters a handful of golden millet along the deck railing and the ground for his little winged friends, smiling at their noisy excitement as a dozen house sparrows eagerly alight from trees and old fence to feast upon the freshly laid buffet.

"Sorry for my absence," he says with genuine sentiment and compassion, a deep affection aglow in his chest.

May all be fed.

These are his rituals of returning. Reorienting. Grounding and centering. Given the day's warmth, he sits outdoors at a mosaic-tiled bistro table, cradling an Asian porcelain cup filled with aromatic jasmine green tea, savouring the heady fragrance and delicate taste. The twittering commotion of happily feeding birds fills him with delight, and occasionally he turns to gaze upward at the trees and filtered sunlight, half-listening to the muffled sounds of the tranquil neighbourhood that surrounds. Resting at ease. Sensing. *Feeling.*

Bodymind still pulses with experiences of the recent travels, a stream of fresh memories playing out, but his rituals comfort and he appreciates the measured downbeats of a familiar, unhurried life. A nomad for too many years, he has no real sense of home, and occasionally he wonders wistfully what it even means or would be like—feeling *home.*

For him, home remains less an actual locale or residence; it is simply *belonging* to a landscape or place, a resonance in one's being more so than particularly deep roots or sense of origin. *Home* is a repeated turning towards that which nurtures his bodysoul while turning away from whatever does not; a sense of balance and comfort, a return to center when life pulls him too far in one direction.

He cherishes sanctuary, yes, whether rented or owned, but home is also in those little rituals and daily celebrations of being human; the moments and actions that bring him back to himself in a conscious, meaningful way—even when deceptively simple, like sweeping the porch. Feeding the birds. Savouring a cup of tea. Cooking dinner. Greeting the dawn.

౭∽

Daylight fades to evening whispers of periwinkle. Using a long, sulfurous matchstick, he lights a dozen candles on the hearth and around the cottage. He turns on some mellow music, pours himself a glass of wine, and sets about creating a modest supper. After two weeks of restaurant fare, how deliciously inviting to cook something *fresh*. His palate craves healthy and flavourful—full of life-force—prepared by his own hands and savoured in a peaceful, non-commercial environment.

Separating sturdy, crisp chard leaves from their rainbow-coloured stalks, he offers a little prayer of gratitude for the freshness in hand. A vital and vibrant gift of good earth.

His meal prepared, he eats silently and alone at the small table by the front window, observing the fading violet sky through a tangled frame of silhouetted tree boughs, the flickering beeswax taper beside him casting a circle of golden illumination like a protective spell. For a moment, a note of blue rings in his wild heart, missing his beloved after the delight of traveling together, and now once again sailing a solitary passage for a while. Unfathomable, the mysterious currents of life.

The bold flavours on his plate—astringent greens, pungent chili and garlic, a kiss of lemon and salt, the earthy and buttered goodness of grains—taste all the more delectable for their organic, fresh simplicity. With a nibble of dark chocolate and a cup of fine tea to follow, all seems right in the world again. Or nearly.

Good, indeed, to enjoy a change of pace and scenery, the excitement of international travel to a realm beyond the everyday familiar and mundane. Yet also how pleasing the return to a simple, quiet life that nourishes and sustains. In the busy, hurried, noisy realms of *doing*, a world of people glued to handheld mobile devices, how essential to *unplug* and revert to a slower, tactile and more connected, non-technological approach to life.

What truly *nourishes* on a deep level, both cellular and spirit? What might we discover when we live at *soul speed* rather than full throttle?

ༀ

Nightfall. A lustrous pearl of moon and diamond stars have emerged, just as each night since the saga of Troy and even further back into mists of timelessness. The man stands barefoot outdoors in the dark beneath the great tree, listening to the primordial chant of the nearby sea, drawing in the salty air scented with resinous cypress and intoxicating, night-blooming jasmine. Gratitude overflows his heart like a golden chalice. Such beauty and uncountable blessings. What grace this earthly, aging body as vessel for the soul. The supreme privilege of being alive, ensconced in bones and breath, on a blue-green jewel of a planet spinning through the vast cosmos. The ordinary sacred in every breath.

Perhaps one day I will find a place in the world to finally call home, he sighs amid the enlivened shadows, feeling the welcome energy of earth underfoot.

Until such day, the modest rituals of returning are like a warm embrace, welcoming him back to hearth and garden. And he knows his own heart is the place where he always has roots nurturing him to grow and bloom—ultimately bearing fruit to offer forward as a gift to the more-than-human world.

❧ ❧ ❧

Opening to Dreams, Inviting the Soul

(January, 2016)

Lying in the darkness, combing through vivid images of a dream from which I have just awakened, the swirl of emotions feels as if I were walking through my daylight hours. Intense. Real.

Reluctantly, I rise from the warmth of our canopied bed, pull on some cozy clothes, and ambulate to the front room of the cottage where I generally greet the day. Still wrapped in the dreamworld's softly textured shawl, I strike a match and am met by its familiar sulfurous hiss. Lighting the two beeswax tapers on the table alongside the front windows, warm spheres of illumination gently push against the shadows beyond the old glass. Crossing to the kitchen, tea kettle is placed atop a blue flame to boil, and I then return to the table with pen and notebook in hand.

Dreams, soul, and the subconscious, each with its own mysterious agenda at work in our lives. Some say *soul* and *subconscious* are the same; semantics and perceived distinctions aside, whatever the case, dreams are a key realm where such guiding forces play out.

For years, a dream journal has rested next to my bed, replaced by a new one when its final page is scribbled upon. Often when I wake in the early morning, or perhaps in the middle of the night, writing by the light of a headlamp/head-torch, if necessary, I record in detail what has arisen in the Dreamtime. Sometime later, usually as I sit with a cup of fine tea, I review the dream: reading it aloud, narrating it slowly in first person and present tense—as if I am experiencing it *now*—and then again, gradually adding in images, feelings, and associations.

Each time I tell it aloud, more of the dream emerges from my depths, along with some surprising connections and intriguing correlations. Avoiding immediate interpretations (and steering well clear of any of those damned dream dictionaries), I let the images continue to subtly work on me throughout the day; summoning them again to my mind's eye whenever I can, permitting myself to float and drift with them. Rather than attempting to just figure it out quickly, I allow the night's puzzling scenario to reveal its deeper layers to me through repeated waking encounters with it. Dream work for me is usually a slow simmer rather than a rapid boil.

Lately, I've not been regularly transcribing my dream matrix adventures but I do continue to work with them, especially when I feel a noticeable emotional charge, or when episodes and scenarios repeat themselves—clear signs that something relevant seeks my attention. Honestly, I dream so actively that there are just too many to work with, even if I wanted to do it daily, and certainly each one doesn't need to be processed.

Many people consider dreams to be simply a neural mishmash of images, or the brain sorting through the day's events and/or unfinished business. However, you'll find me decidedly in the camp that values dreaming as more than that. The Dreamtime is a primary aperture to the soul, and it beckons every one of us, even if we don't consciously remember the narratives when we wake each morning. Psychology "depth therapy" approaches to dream interpretation often hold that every aspect of the milieu—each character, object, and image—represents an element of ourselves (albeit cleverly disguised), even objects like an apple, a broken window, a skeleton, or a naked friend. This is partly what makes interpretation such a fascinating, revealing puzzle.

Dreams are powerful, cryptic invitations to slip into the currents of subconscious *longing*—often more an abduction than solicitation. The Aborigines, as well as other native First Peoples and wisdom traditions, believe that beyond the nightly initiation of the soul, the Dreamtime offers a portal to other dimensions and parallel realities. My own experience concurs with their long-held truths, for at night I cross over into realms that simply cannot be accessed during the day, even in heightened states of awareness.

Everything is real.

Not long ago, in a powerful, archetypal "message" dream, I glimpsed the Dreammaker; an Asian goddess-like figure whose long dark hair fell in a braid down her back, seated gracefully erect at a round table, slender-handled paintbrushes at hand, each smooth stroke bridging realities and destiny. Simple as it may sound, this was a *very* powerful experience; it felt like a privileged peek into the workings of the cosmos. As if she really chooses and paints my dreams (with everyone else's), I heed her messages, cryptic as they may be. And somehow I discern when the scenario and story holds portent, as if it speaks louder somehow, triggering a knowing in my bodymind. *Yes ... trust this.*

Over and over, I offer that each of us has something essential to offer the world, such being the journey of the soul. Stepping even further into realms of mystery, what if Earth and Cosmos are *dreaming us*, nudging people towards their unique gifts and destiny, conspiring to bring humanity awake as part of the great evolutionary arc and spiral...?

Call it what you will—Source, One, Mystery, Great Spirit, God, Consciousness—but the *Unnameable* communicates in myriad ways: via nature and people; curious signs, serendipitous situations, and intersections of fate; dreams, both nighttime and waking; places on the planet that allure and evoke a resonance within us; mysterious synchronicity; wild animals or images that repeatedly present themselves; our creativity and imagination; and the somatic impulses of longing that serve as the soul's compass.

On the hamster wheel of modern life, the majority of people are not listening or paying attention. They simply spin in place, trudge along, or race through a technologically tranced-out world; wondering what's missing, wired to phones and computers while ignoring the signs all around. Mostly we've discarded the soul's longing as too farfetched and idealistic, childish, risky, or impossible. The covers are pulled over our heads and we are not remembering—or even considering—the dream.

Winter has descended here in the northern world, ushering us into the annual passage of long, dark incubation and quiet magic. Now is the time to become the bear who enters his den to rest and dream ... while *being dreamed* in return. Something grows within; gestating as it slowly takes form, a living thing. Hope. Visions. Creativity. And always the soul, summoning us to be in communion with something larger.

Repeatedly I ask myself, to what am I listening and paying attention to in life? Is there something I'm overlooking or not acknowledging that perhaps I ought to be? Where, and towards what, are my dreams and soul steering me... or am I veering away?

This morning in January darkness, enfolded by a hushed cottage and aided by the soft illumination of flickering candles, I sit and write in a "stream of conscious" manner—uncensored, free flow—regarding the dream from which I just woke. Allowing it to spill forward in a jumble of images, connections, and emotions scrawled onto a page. Acknowledging and appreciating the cryptic storyline with its strong emotions as a valuable message, even if, upon first consideration, it seems largely unintelligible.

Cosmic Mind reaches out to us in the dream matrix, issuing an imaginative, enigmatic summons. There is a Larger Story. As surely as we are dreaming, we are also *dreamed*—invited to step into growth and expansion versus fear and constriction, to offer our unique gifts and talents to the more-than-human world. To consciously participate—just like a lucid dream—in humanity's evolution.

When the Dreamtime retreats and we move blearily and busily into our daylight hours, we either carry the messages forward as clues or imperatives, or discard and forget them in the mists—replaced by "to do" lists and the morning's pressing demands. So, too, with the waking dream of our precious lives: each day brings an opportunity to work towards embodying a life of authentic and soulful meaning, of creating goodness and sharing beauty. Or we may set the challenge aside amid the noise, distractions, and well-spun illusions of society, much to the cost of one's own soul.

Don't go back to sleep.

Dance. Sing. Write. Build. Create. Dream. Do. Heal. Risk the thing you've always longed to try or has terrified you. Given you have but one "wild and precious life," what will you do with it?

Just possibly, if you're still looking for and wondering what may be yours to bring, the Dreammaker in her mysterious way will help you find the winding path.

❧ ❧ ❧

The Scent of Green Chile: A Cook's Delight

(September 2015)

The chiles are here.

So proclaims the large sign out front of Whole Foods Market in Monterey, California, beside a table piled high with oblong green peppers from Hatch, New Mexico. On a late August afternoon, my thoughts had been elsewhere until this moment, turning over some detail or matter at hand as I crossed the car park, a reusable jute grocery bag tucked under one arm.

Arrested by the sign and table of glistening chiles piled high, my heart did a happy flip flop inside my chest. Little in the world of food so powerfully conjures for me a sense of place, a feeling of beneficial well-being—the goodness of hearth and home—as do these slender, long emeralds from New Mexico (the ruby ones, too). The familiar smell of their roasting outdoors, rotating in a gas-fired metal drum at a farmer's market or elsewhere, is enough to send me doing cartwheels.

Like the resinous piñon incense that I adore, the aroma of these chiles evokes a locale that I deeply love, yet their familiar scent also transports me to a certain season there. A harbinger of late summer's end, the harvest is upon us and autumn soon arriving.

Fall, as Americans call it, is my favorite season. Not only for its welcome cool and gloriously painted leaves, the gentle sense of melancholy and turning inwards, but also its bounty: crisp apples and juicy pears, hefty squashes and tasty game birds, fresh nuts and wild mushrooms. I celebrate the shift in my own appetite and cooking that occurs this time of year, returning once more to warming soups and stews simmered slowly over a quiet flame, the slow-braised dishes that nearly collapse when you dip into them. I ease back towards red wine rather than white or the dry Provençal rosé I savor all summer long. I hunger for a perfect duck *confit*. Likewise, my signature *Tarte Tatin* with golden puff pastry, as decadent an apple dish as can be.

And then there are chiles. Fabulous chiles. Commonly known as *chili peppers*, "chile" (the Spanish spelling) prevails in the American Southwest and along much of the West Coast. *Hatch peppers*, these green ones are sometimes called—named for the place in New Mexico where they are notably grown (and arguably the best). Nowadays they are cultivated widely elsewhere, including California and

Arizona, and there are both hot and mild varieties. Ortega is a well-known brand of canned green chiles (most of them *not* grown in Hatch, NM), serving as a popular condiment in Mexican food and New Mexican cuisine, though as with anything in industrial tins, the flavor doesn't compare to fresh.

Green or red, spicy or tame, regional chiles form the base of salsas and sauces, and contribute an essential element to traditional New Mexico dishes like *posole*—typically a lamb stew with hominy (lime-cured white corn) and chiles. Loads of chiles.

℘

Right food, right place, right time. It's a philosophy of good cooks everywhere, celebrating what is in-season, local and fresh. I suppose one could argue that eating New Mexico capsicums on the central California coast doesn't strictly qualify as right *place*, though both the *food* and *time* are certainly perfect. These shiny jewels are the genuine article from Hatch, New Mexico, fresh and seasonal... and I am buying them for supper.

Yes, they traveled across two states to reach me, and not that I need any justification, but the overwhelming majority of what I purchase *is* grown locally. (I am cognizant that such a stance is relatively easy on the Left Coast of the States where so much of the country's fresh produce is grown.)

Last autumn, on one of my writing retreats before I relocated to this coastal peninsula, Whole Foods Market briefly had genuine Hatch chiles and I excitedly scooped handfuls into a large bag. They were not marked as hot or mild, and it didn't matter to me; I greedily consume them all. Back at the cottage, after roasting some of my haul, I discovered they were quite spicy—far too fiery for my mate's taste. (Sorry, love.)

Personally, I'm inclined to buy a bucketload and put them in and on *everything*: punctuating a creamy quiche, and stuffing them whole with other ingredients, making salsa and deeply warming stews. Twice I've resided in New Mexico, and while my painted gypsy wagon has rolled far from the landscape that endures as a spiritual touchstone, these chiles remain *soul food* for a wanderer.

This evening I am cooking for my mother-in-law (it's Sunday dinner), who isn't overly fond of spicy food. Recalling last year's fiery bite and how my partner's head almost blew off, reluctantly I decide the peppers will be a side event rather than the star of the show. *Sigh*. Restraining my ecstatic, gluttonous self, I place just a handful into a small brown paper sack, and will serve them alongside the soft-shell chicken tacos I'll prepare.

At home, after laying a few chiles on a cast-iron grill pan atop a medium-high flame, their familiar, slightly pungent perfume begins to waft up and fill the kitchen. It's culinary incense for me... heaven. *Oh, yes*. Maybe I will eat them all tonight, irrespective.

Whether as cooks or simply *eaters*, likely each of us has some sort of ingredient or dish that triggers a positive association with time and place, be it childhood nostalgia or an adult culinary appreciation. Other ingredients excite and inspire me—a freshly-caught fish with eyes still glistening, a prized black truffle, a gorgeous pheasant, a bunch of anything fragrant and fresh from the garden—but few have the ability to catapult this chef to a place that instills a sense of home, deep contentment, and well-being.

※

After blackening the chiles in the hot pan (just as easily they could be blistered under a broiler, on a gas grill, or over an open flame), I transfer them to a favorite French earthenware *tian,* and tightly seal the top with cling film for a few minutes to sweat their skins loose. Not so long as to let them overcook and get soggy. Peeling away the thin green parchment in long strips with my fingers, I remove the fibrous center ribs and scrape out the abundance of flat white seeds—elements which contain the highest concentration of the compound that delivers the "heat." A gentle sprinkling of flaky salt crushed between my fingertips and we're all set for gustatory bliss. A wet kiss of lemon or lime could stage a further seduction, but here and now I'm a purist being prim.

Plates of supper in hand, stepping out onto the deck, the coastal air is cool enough to warrant my well-worn blue hoodie. First notes of autumn play upon the breeze. Seated at the tiled bistro table with my guest, I bite into a taco, relishing the interplay of organic corn tortilla, spice-rubbed free-range chicken, and the avocado-tomato salsa (flecked with cilantro, chipotle, and fresh lime) of which I could eat a bowl full. Yet it is the distinctive, roasted green chile that compels me to close my eyes and momentarily swoon with delight.

For the briefest moment, I am transported to the high desert plateau of Taos where the air is perfumed with sagebrush; to the Santa Fe Farmers Market, my Paris basket loaded with fresh bounty from the familiar weekly vendors; to the High Country of New Mexico mountains where shimmering aspens illuminate the slopes, turning them to brilliant, flaming gold. Returning to my past, I am tucked indoors at a rustic wooden table, beneath the roughly-hewn ceiling *vigas* of an old, adobe house while piñon logs burn on the hearth of a kiva fireplace.

Yet, simultaneously, I am fully in the moment—savoring a meal of bold flavors beneath the sheltering boughs of the Grandmother Monterey cypress on a cool, end of summer evening. Such goodness of life. A modest celebration of the most tasteful sort. Exquisite, really.

☙

What feeds the soul?

I'm repeatedly putting forth that query in this weekly column, and if you read these posts even somewhat regularly you probably know my answer: soul nourishment comes through living with our senses wide open, welcoming those little, ordinary moments of the day—ones that, if we are paying attention, are sensual celebrations of being *fully* human. They are the cornerstones of life as a Soul Artist.

Nature always reflects our soul—arguably, it IS our soul—and offers uncountable blessings to us. Similarly, good and honest food from the mindfully-tended earth (or foraged wild) also nourishes us deeply. As a cook, I am keenly attuned to the grace of the table, delighted by the gifts of each season, and find joy in sharing with others whenever I may.

Summer in the Northern Hemisphere is ending; the bright days shorten and begin to thin their light, while a slow turning inward begins. First offerings of the next seasonal passage arrive daily. Let's celebrate, I say, for doing so is the very soul of humanity.

And let there be chiles.

❧ ❧ ❧

The Day As A Grown Man I Met My Birthmother
(September 2015)

This post was written after a lengthy deliberation whether or not I would say yes to the suggestion of a senior editor at the **Good Men Project** *who has two adopted boys. I did not initially intend to share the piece as one of my weekly Soul Artist Journal offerings, feeling it was more of a personal story (with a restricted word count) rather than related to a soulful life for the senses. Ultimately, my feeling changed and I decided to offer it forward, after all. ~*

I sat in my car, parked outside her residence—the very house I'd already driven past a dozen times in the past week, hoping I wouldn't be seen. My body buzzed with nervousness, a current of energy in my core so intense that I nearly shook.

It was my thirty-sixth birthday, and I was about to meet my birthmother for the first time since I entered the world.

On a tree-shaded street in a pleasant neighborhood of Portland, Oregon, I stepped from my green Ford Explorer and walked to the front door of her modest bungalow. My heart pounded like a great drum, so fiercely and fast I thought it might burst from my chest. I inhaled a deep breath, straightened my buttoned-down shirt, and summoned all my courage. Then I knocked on the door.

A moment later, it swung open and I was greeted by a tall, slender woman with short silver hair. She stood with poise, a tailored skirt and blouse accenting her shapely form. Angled cheekbones and flawless pale skin framed the dark brown pools of her eyes. At sixty-three she was strikingly beautiful; in her youth she must have been absolutely stunning.

We have the same eyes, I realized, and something like a cry broke open inside me, catching at the back of my throat. I swallowed hard.

A long, silent moment passed as we regarded each other across the threshold. For the very first time in my life, I gazed at a face that resembled my own. I *looked like* someone ... like my birth mother.

❧

Adopted children have no birth story. Our life begins the day we came home from the agency or the orphanage. We never hear how many hours our mother struggled in labor, or "You have your father's chin." Similarly, we don't possess Uncle Charley's nose or Grandmother's temperament. Our true biological heritage remains a mystery, often hidden one's entire life.

As I trembled on the doorstep like a teenager rather than a grown man, Katherine invited me inside. Hoping my voice wouldn't crack, I stepped into the house as a dozen emotions surged like waves crashing together within me.

This face-to-face moment was the dramatic conclusion of a lengthy process: an opening of court records, a subsequent long and frustrated seeking on my part; a paid, assisted search in cooperation with the adoption agency, yielding a notification that she was willing to meet me; an exchange of letters; and finally, her suggestion that we have lunch on my upcoming birthday.

❧

My eyes swept the surroundings, trying to somehow glean a sense of this woman who, at twenty-seven brought me into the world—and then without ever seeing her child, relinquished me to another life. Scanning her porcelain face, the modestly appointed house, I looked for clues about her ... about me. Were we alike in any way?

We sat in the simply furnished living room. Similar to my own dwelling, the fireplace mantle and built-in bookcases were decorated with worthless treasures gathered from nature: pinecones, sea shells, unusual rocks of various hues and shapes, bits of driftwood. As in my house, there was a total absence of family photos.

"I suppose you want to know something of your birth father," she said, matter of factly. "You look a bit like him."

Withholding his name, she spoke briefly of their affair; he a married man who went back to his wife when he learned Katherine was pregnant. Telling the story all these years later, her anger still simmered like a blue flame, turned up high at the end with a vindictive comment. A scorpion's sting. Her enduring bitterness startled me. What a long time to carry a heavy sword, I thought. And yet, how long have I denied and wrestled with my own buried anger?

၄৩

We walked a few blocks to the place she had chosen to have lunch, a community house and garden, and sat across from each other in wooden, high back chairs. Mother and adult son meeting for the first time, our meal together had all the nervousness and awkwardness of a first date.

From the letters exchanged, we already knew the brief, vague outlines of each other's life: siblings, children, schooling, and work in the world. Yet I learned on that first lunch that I was actually the second child she had placed for adoption. Four years previous to my birth, at twenty-three she gave up her first child; she knew nothing of him. Her third son, born fourteen years after me, was of her current marriage, and she said he was eager to meet me.

Katherine had long been interested in astrology and considered herself something of an expert. As a birthday present, she prepared my birth chart and printed it on purple paper. While we sat at lunch, she read the chart aloud, describing me in somewhat eerie detail, pointing out my various challenges and shortcomings. I wanted to feel grateful for the gift, but mostly I found myself feeling both naked and exposed.

Throughout our meal, I was struck by her keen, obvious intelligence and deliberate, articulate speech. She was friendly but reserved, cool rather than warm. Her straight posture and continuous poise—even the way she held her fork and chewed her food—was a closer sibling to *rigidity* than *grace*.

Those flashing dark eyes regarded me intently, considering each word I spoke and every gesture I made. Measuring me. My sense of her was of a wild falcon or hawk. Beautiful. Solitary. Aloof and seemingly docile on her perch, at any moment she might launch with flashing talons to swoop upon her prey and tear it apart.

၄৩

After our meal, we ambled through the neighborhood back to her house where, at the front porch, she announced that she wouldn't be inviting me in. She had other things to do but we could meet again in the future. For a moment, I was taken aback; not simply by her bluntness or the solidity of the boundary, but because it was *exactly* the sort of thing I would say and do—like gazing into a mirror.

We exchanged a light, tentative hug and I returned to my car. She went into the house and closed the door.

I had met my birthmother. Searching for her was one of the most significant things I've ever done in my life. In meeting, some missing piece of the puzzle inside of me finally snapped into place with a nearly audible click.

I look like someone.

As I drove away, trying to stay afloat in a whirlpool of powerful emotions, what engulfed me was *gratitude;* not that Katherine and I had finally met, but rather that she had given me up and I had been fortunate enough to be raised by good-hearted parents who loved and celebrated me.

What a curious, unexpected twist. Such grace.

Warm tears streaming down my face, I found myself awash in appreciation for my adoptive mother, departed from the earth, who steered me continually towards my own soul. What a priceless gift to be loved, to be wanted, to be cherished as one's own son.

A hundred-thousand blessings to everyone who adopts a child. Straight, gay, mixed-race, it doesn't matter; *love* makes a family.

The May afternoon I met my birthmother was the day that, regardless of bloodline, I rediscovered my true family—the two special people who brought me home from the adoption agency and my life really began.

❧ ❧ ❧

A Heart Open to the World: Finding Beauty
(November, 2015)

An autumn morning shines brightly blue, warm enough that the light jacket and linen scarf I have brought aren't needed. Seated upon an old wooden bench worn grey from years of exposure to the coastal elements, I am a creature contentedly bathing in sunlight and ocean breezes.

Just half an hour ago, comfortably ensconced in my small writer's cottage, I appreciated the sunny morning through wide front widows, savoring my ritual pot of morning tea. In true confession, I was avoiding the work of writing an article for an online publication, feeling stymied and uninspired. Then the knowing part of me whispered, something of a prod, *go walk the shoreline trail.* Doubtless, going outdoors and walking, preferably barefoot, would not only realign my entire perspective but also give me words for the piece. Not to mention shifting my biochemistry and nourishing my wild soul. In less than ten minutes, I was out the door with my small day pack, the tea cup washed and placed on the bamboo drying rack, while the Sussex Duo, my two English Whippets, looked forlorn with big brown eyes at being left behind.

I am terribly fond of this spot where I now sit and write, just south of town and easy to reach yet tucked away from the tourists. The weather-worn bench feels like an old friend, ever a fine place to watch the ever-shifting waves not ten yards from my feet, observing noisy white seagulls and California brown pelicans, along with the occasional sea otter floating on its back amid tangled ribbons of salty kelp. I have perched here in all sorts of weather and moods, resting for mere moments or the better part of an afternoon, entranced by the soul-stirring beauty. Listening to the song of the world, feeling my own being as a note in that harmonic chorus.

It has been a week of travels, of world violence, and a lingering sense of grief for a place I have lived and loved—The City of Lights, dear Paris of my heart. Feeling tender, I am grateful to be home at my little sanctuary, nurtured in body and spirit by familiar surroundings and the simple rituals that comprise my daily life: greeting the morning outdoors with bare feet on the earth; feeding the birds; sweeping the deck of Monterey cypress needles; a pot of English tea and morning writing by the front windows; the smoky scent of resinous piñon incense; walking the dogs through our tree-filled neighborhood; puttering in the kitchen to soft music as I construct a meal of fresh ingredients for supper; seated on a sheepskin before my Navajo loom with hand-spun *churro* yarns; candlelight in the evenings;

a nourishing book.

Weekly in this column, I endeavor to share something of a quiet, hand-fashioned life lived deliberately, if not always the sacrifices for such an existence. Despite my focus on soulful nourishment, still today there is heartache for the places rocked in senseless violence and lives torn apart. Sometimes it seems Shadow mentality has run amok in the world, that humanity will never really evolve. Some days I am strong enough and my heart large enough to hold the entire world and its suffering, while other times I simply can't take one more measure of sadness.

I cannot mend a broken, angry, misguided world. All I can do is open heart and senses more widely and turn toward the things that are beautiful—like the reddish orange and black butterfly that flutters nearby, erratically navigating the marine breeze. The churning foam of sapphire waves in a timeless symphony of elemental music. The crumbly cool earth beneath my bare soles, and the rusty tint of the fleshy ice plants, these ground-hugging succulent perennials everywhere around where I sit.

Here, now, welcome the beauty.

Such a dance, this. Leaning into the heartache—whether of the world or our own lives—allowing ourselves to feel grief deeply but also turning toward beauty and goodness. Holding the tension of duality. Like standing outdoors in the pale dawn with arms outstretched in opposite directions, a rising sun in one open hand and setting moon in the other.

What I know deep inside is that each of us has something to bring to the 'more-than-human' world, an offering that emerges from the soul. The journey of a lifetime is discovering what such gift may be, its curious shape and reflective facets, and then finding ways to give it forward with abandon. Without shame. Some days, it feels that I fail miserably, falling far short of what I long to accomplish and share, finding myself tangled in disappointments and silken blues.

Then I step outside and remember, for my eyes and heart always turn toward beauty, however humble and small. I marvel at the purple flowering sage illuminated in morning sun, calling me near. Or a snowy jasmine blossom. The fuzzy black and yellow caterpillar inching along the fence. The hum and flash of an emerald hummingbird. The iridescent gleam of sunlight on the thorax of a large black beetle. A humble green weed or dandelion. Truly, the list of my allurements could be endless.

So often the most ordinary, simple things are the most beautiful.

Yet so few of us are paying attention—*really* noticing what is around us. And even fewer heed the whispers of their wild soul, that core essence seeking ever to expand in communion with something much larger and timeless. Or simply the sensuality of this fleeting, gilded moment.

Here on the weathered oceanside bench, my senses revel in a mélange of colors, scents, tastes, textures, and feelings that enfold me. I'm almost drunk on the beauty—if not actually intoxicated, most definitely under the influence of the Wild Beloved at the edge of a continent.

Meanwhile, the world goes on.

There will be struggle and doubt, grief and loss. We will forget, remember, and forget again. It's simply part of the human journey, frustrating as it may be, enfolding us all in our respective realities.

Soon I will lay aside my trusty old fountain pen from Paris, the notebook too, and just sit for a while as briny air and a flashing sea seeps into my soul, nourishing me to the core. Then I will return to my rented, down-at-heel cottage, open the red front door wide to the late morning and day, welcoming the chatter of birds and a soft breeze whispering in the trees, as I go about my work—striving to offer some small measure of beauty to the world, however I might.

It is good and right to shed tears for the world, I think, but may we weep also for its staggering beauty. Everywhere. And if you cannot find beauty in what surrounds you, go in search of it. Create it with your hands and heart, and then give it away selflessly. Freely. Madly. Even if it's just a song. A poem. A story. Perhaps a garden. Or a simple supper for your beloved.

Heal the heart by finding and offering beauty. And kindness. Gratitude, too. We are only here a short while, after all.

Breathing in, breathing out...

The true, highest nature of humanity is *grace*, even amid shadows and heartbreak. Perhaps especially then. *Always grace,* I say, offering both a prayer and blessing. Friend, may it come to you wrapped in beauty.

                         ea ea ea

Greeting the Holy

(October, 2015)

In coastal morning air amid the trees, the high desert plateau of New Mexico seems a world away. I have returned from a retreat to dear Taos, my former haunt at the foot of a sacred mountain, welcomed by this small writer's cottage where I currently dwell. Here at the edge of a continent, an alluring threshold of earth, sea and sky, I am slowly changing shape—waiting for my soul to find its way home from wanderings and catch me up.

The sky sings a melody of soft blue as the tall green conifers reach to catch hold of it. Barefoot for *earthing*, a corn fiber broom in my hand, I rhythmically sweep away the brown-green pellets of Monterey cypress needles that have carpeted the deck, bricks, and walkway in my absence.

I rose late this morning after yesterday's travels, emerging from the house to greet the day in my usual way: a standing, mini-meditation, my barefoot ritual of sole to soil. A quiet opportunity to offer thanks and gratitude, to toss intentions and prayers to the firmament like the golden millet I scatter on the deck railing for the little birds that delight me. Stepping out to greet the holy in everything.

Sweeping becomes its own ritual, the everyday sacred embodied, breathing in and out with unclad feet upon the cool wood and bricks. *Whsssk, whsssk, whsssk ...*

I hear them before seeing them and immediately look up. My eyes scan the pale blue sky through the trees as heart launches on wings in my chest, responding to the sound of wild geese honking in flight. Through the shapely boughs of the venerable Grandmother they materialize: six Canadian geese in a V-formation, flying low and calling out.

How wonderful and curious. Not that an abundance of wild geese aren't around, especially at the Carmel River and wetlands sanctuary at the shoreline, but my cottage is a mile north of there, and I don't usually see or hear them over the town.

Broom in hand, I watch their passage south on rapidly beating wings, voices calling to my soul in an autumnal song and invoking a wordless cry of jubilation in reply. Instantly, my heart's tone shifts and becomes "Wild Geese" by the poet Mary Oliver, words summoned by the waterfowl themselves.

You do not have to be good.
You do not have to walk on your knees
for a hundred miles through the desert, repenting.
You have only to let the soft animal of your body
love what it loves.
Tell me about despair, yours, and I will tell you mine.
Meanwhile the world goes on.
Meanwhile the sun and clear pebbles of rain
are moving across the landscapes,
over the prairies and deep trees,
the mountains and rivers.
Meanwhile, the wild geese, high in the clean blue air,
are heading home again.
Whoever you are, no matter how lonely,
the world offers itself to your imagination,
calls to you like the wild geese, harsh and exciting—
over and over announcing your place
in the family of things.

I know Oliver's words by heart. Her classic poem is among the first ones I chose to learn and carry inside to always have with me, offering comfort and inspiration wherever I may roam.

A poem spoken aloud is a wondrous thing. Even more powerful when it inhabits the heart like a lover or old friend, effortlessly recalled from memory. Inviting soulful poems to take up residence in my being is something of a *soul practice*. Admittedly, I haven't yet memorized many, perhaps twenty; some are brief, others lengthy. "Wild Geese" is always there in my pocket like a green stone rubbed smooth from wishing upon it.

Meanwhile the world goes on.

Hearing the geese as I sweep the bricks and deck feels like a different sort of welcome home than the coyotes of Taos in last week's journal post. Once again I am reminded of the goodness of this place where I reside. *Be here now.* It's a neighborhood, yes, and hardly wild as I long for, but quiet enough at night and early mornings, when I step out to gaze at the moon or greet the day, I can hear the low, rumbling voice of the sea less than a mile distant.

Meanwhile, the wild geese, high in the clean blue air / are heading home again.

Soul, come home. Be here and at peace. Sit by the brick hearth and watch the daylight fade through westerly windows as the pastel mysteries of dusk gather close with timeless, hushed voices.

When I first met Oliver's poem years ago, I loved the initial lines—her encouragement to be in my body and let that soft, sensual animal-nature love what it loves. In the decade since, as I have deepened into relationship with those wild geese, I've come to cherish the closing stanza equally to the beginning.

Much of my life has been spent searching for my place in the world. Some elusive locale where I feel at home, nourished by both nature *and* culture—the place where my human beloved feels the same—while I continue to discover what is uniquely mine to bring and offer. As a nomad, threshold dweller, and reluctant mystic, sometimes it is a solitary journey, even in the warm comfort of intimate relationship with a good-hearted mate.

Wild geese passing overhead on a crisp autumn morning in a quiet little, tree-filled town by the sea. Unexpected messengers of mystery and soul. Comforting and reminding me, *your life is not elsewhere, River.* Dream. Create. Breathe in this moment with senses cast wide, a broom in hand, feeling earth under bare soles and a heart echoing with poems and beauty.

Whoever you are, no matter how lonely / the world offers itself to your imagination...

I stepped out to greet the holy, connect to cool soil with unclad feet, and sweep the porch. If "holy" seems a tricky word, we might instead say "sacred." Call it *intelligence.* Or simply pause to marvel and awe, realizing we are greeted and witnessed in return—everything from glistening spider web to laughing crows to fading blossom on the tangled vine.

How lovely to be welcomed by the sanctuary of a place, the smile and warmth of a beloved, by wild things of the 'more-than-human' world. To find a poem rising in the heart.

Friend, you are inseparable from all that surrounds. For not only does the world offer itself to our imagination, each of us is part of such *imagining itself.*

Here. Now. Breathe in, breathe out, feet firmly upon the earth as a mutual blessing of reciprocity and goodness.

And if only in this heartbeat of a moment, may you *celebrate* your place in the family of things.

❧ ❧ ❧

The Art of Slow Food: Duck à la Marlena

(December, 2015)

A dmittedly, here is some extravagance. One could say it brings new meaning to *slow food*, both the cooking term and foodie culinary movement.

Setting out to make a dish of duck requiring nine days isn't your everyday undertaking. Surely it's fit only for a holiday, or a prince, and in our rushed and harried world, perhaps not even that. Overnight marks the upper limit of what most cooks would be willing to invest, perhaps a day or two if the project is largely unattended (as with a true *levain* bread). Nine days?! Please, it's almost ridiculous.

This folly of a fowl first nested in my head as I read the latest offering from Marlena de Blasi, an American expat who has made Italy her home for over twenty years. I discovered her memoirs whilst living in England, and was immediately smitten by their lushly gilded prose. The old-fashioned sensibilities, her attunement to the sensuality of life, and glorious descriptions of the regional food of her adopted country captivated me. Last May, in a million-to-one twist of fate, I met Marlena at an iconic Left Bank café in Paris, as relayed in the SAJ post "A Paris Encounter: Meeting de Blasi" [included in the first SAJ compilation, *To Kneel and Kiss the Earth*]. That meeting launched a correspondence and subsequently blossoming friendship, and she promised to send her soon-to-be-released work, *The Umbrian Thursday Night Supper Club*. True to her word, a few weeks later the signed, hardcover book arrived from overseas—along with an Italian tin of home-baked, divine goodness in the form of a salty-sweet, biscotti-like confection.

Like her other books, this latest offering is a window into a simpler, traditional life gradually disappearing. The story centers upon the friendship forged between five women over a ritual of Thursday night suppers, concocted in a rustic stone building with an open fire. Cooking and eating together, the narrative weaves the personal histories that have shaped them, with Marlena dancing between confidant, friend, and the outsider even after two decades in Italy. The tale celebrates unpretentious Italian fare sourced close to home or foraged wild, making do with whatever is to hand and in season—along with the bonding of hearts over shared meals, especially as de Blasi draws each woman forward to share her gifts, recipes, and secrets.

Toward the end of the book, Marlena entwines the recipe for a nine-day duck with the story of her friend, Gilda, who has enquired about and wants to make the dish.

As ingredients and method unfolded throughout the chapter, I thought, *I must prepare and eat this*, jotting down scribbled notes as I turned the pages. Not only do I adore duck but the cook in me—French-trained and decidedly a do-it-by-hand, old fashioned soul—was utterly intrigued by something that requires even longer to make than my weeklong duck *confit*, a perennial favorite I undertake each autumn. Add to this the promise in dialogue between Marlena and Gilda, the dish would be so tender it could be eaten with a spoon, bathed in a beguilingly complex sauce, well, nothing further need be said.

Upon finishing *The Umbrian Thursday Night Supper Club*, I wrote to Chou (as Marlena insists I call her), "I swear to you, I am going to make that drunken duck."

Flash forward a couple of months. Upon returning from some travels, as the colours, scents, and gently crisp days of November on the central California coast again enfolded me, I decided it was time to undertake *le canard*. The dish would be a festive meal for the approaching holidays—though given the date of my return to this cottage and the nine days of its preparation it wouldn't be ready for Thanksgiving dinner. No matter. Let it be a private celebration for my beloved and me.

Among her other books, Marlena is the author of two cookbooks on regional Italian food. I have enough affinity for her culinary palette (and palate) that I was willing to plunge in, confident the result would be worth the investment both in time and money (a pricey duck, multiple bottles of wine, etc.). She has a fondness for combinations of salty and sweet, and perhaps equally for savoury and sweet; this dish was clearly the latter. Bring on the duck. A free range, organic, never frozen one, thank you. Make it two, actually.

❧

American cooking icon, Julia Child, once quipped, "Noncooks think it's silly to invest two hours' work in two minutes' enjoyment; but if cooking is evanescent, well, so is the ballet." I couldn't agree more. Unabashedly, I confess to a deep enjoyment of the gathering and shopping, washing, chopping, prepping, simmering, etcetera. You enjoy it or you don't, and I say it is the mark of a real cook to be in the first camp rather than the latter.

Still, can anything possibly be worth a nine-day preparation and wait? I endeavored to relinquish expectations and simply enjoy the process for itself—which, after the first seven days of curing in salt and herbs, is mostly a repeated braising in different wines interspersed with overnight resting. A few additions and then reductions of the sauce. Nothing about the actual method or ingredients is beyond the reach of a basic home cook.

As Marlena says, it wants for time rather than trouble—which to me seems the very essence of *slow food*, delivering a much needed antidote to our rushed life and fast, anonymous fare. I would offer that something built slowly and deliberately embodies the best notion of *artisan,* a term so watered down and misapplied in the food world—applied without irony or shame to Safeway bread and Starbucks sandwiches, for example—that it has generally lost its meaning.

When the autumn moon waxed full and began to wane, I would content myself in sitting down at last to savour something on which time had been lavished in a quiet ritual of good taste. Perhaps a glass of rosé Champagne or Crémant d'Alsace alongside—the holidays are arriving, after all. (Not that one *ever* needs an excuse for nice bubbly in a crystal flute.)

When I am not working with clients, or pushing a pen and stringing words together, my life tends to revolve around the kitchen. Certainly, it's the heart of our home, my everyday *atelier* for nourishing body and soul. Yet even in a quiet existence, I'm often haunted by the longing for an even quieter, simpler time and slower pace, where days are interwoven with a deep sense of place amid the beauty of nature. Certainly, I cannot change the world, but I make deliberate choices that allow me to spend time in the kitchen, cooking something gently on the stove or in the oven, and eventually placing a fragrant or fresh dish of something on the table as a modest celebration. Every day.

Investing time into food, choosing the freshest, finest ingredients we can buy and treating those with care and love, yields fare that is something better than *artisan* or even gourmet. *Honest food,* I call it, a deeply nourishing balm for body and soul. Healing, even.

Soul Artists know that a nourishing existence doesn't merely happen of its own accord, it is cultivated and tended. Such a life entails deliberate actions in our busy, profane world. One has to make time for the little rituals that sustain us on a deep level, like cooking a lovely meal for ourselves and beloved(s), food that consoles and comforts. Or a walk outdoors amid the falling, withered leaves, warmly bundled up with senses cast wide, celebrating the polysensory experience of inhabiting the moment, delighting in what it offers. *Everything is connected.*

So often I query in this column, to what will we give the gift of time, attention and care? If it doesn't sound too grandiose, how might we feed the Soul of the World—from which we are never separate—even if that is simply the meal upon our plates.

❦

Of course, my nine-day dish doesn't taste the way Marlena's does. Rather it is the result of where I dwell, the local duck and fresh thyme, different shallots and pancetta than in Italy, New World wine versus Old World, and my own hands with their innate sense of how things should be measured and taste. Interpretations and improvisations, moods and weather. The outcome is as much a product of this foggy stretch of coastline as of my own intentions and heart while I tended the slow process, scattering blessings over it like seasonings, silent prayers whispered into the fragrantly rising steam.

A pair of golden beeswax tapers on the table flickering against the darkness of the chilly night beyond the windows, we finally sat down to eat the long awaited dish.

"Oh my God," swooned my mate taking the first bite.

Served in a wide-rimmed white bowl and bathed in the dark ruby sauce, crowned by pancetta and shallots from the cooking process, the drunken duck breast was both rustic and elegant. As promised by Marlena and Gilda in the book, it was meltingly tender, the complex juices both savoury and sweet. Rich, *oh yes.*

This is truly the kind of cuisine worth eating slowly, luxuriating with eyes closed, and lingering unhurriedly at the table. Indeed, to rush through a meal that has taken more than a week to emerge from the kitchen would be disgraceful. The winey duck was just what I hoped it would be: a *slow food* celebration of life, a perfect prelude to the approaching year-end holidays.

"It was worth every bite," I wrote to Chou a few days afterward.

"My sincere appreciation to that duck," she responded. "It makes me miss Gilda. I will tell you about her someday."

Marlena has recently invited me to her home in Umbria to cook and bake together, an utterly delicious opportunity. Who knows, perhaps she will choose to tell me about her friend when we visit, maybe while sipping a glass of local wine, strolling a bustling outdoor market, or sitting with a cappuccino. I would welcome any stories as a gift. For now, I am content with the lavish duck, feeling grateful that souls like Marlena remain in the world—ones who uphold that a nine-day investment in supper isn't absurd but worthwhile. Necessary, even.

Mirroring her comment, I offer countless blessings of thanks to the dear fowl, for all the other ingredients involved, along with the unknown hands that tended, gathered and delivered them into my reach. As conscious human beings, is it not our role to honour the people, places and things that enrich our lives, to appreciate and acknowledge their effect upon us? Surely it is. May I move through my days with such a spirit of praise and gratitude as I gather, cook, write—offering what I can to the world in return.

Candles aglow in the window against the dark night, let the winter holidays begin. Slowly. Unhurriedly. Perhaps simmered softly with good wine, and long steeped in savoury-sweet gratitude.

❧ ❧ ❧

For any who may find the idea of this leisurely dish appealing and worth a try, here is the basic outline I lifted and compiled from the pages of Gilda's story in The Umbrian Thursday Night Supper Club. *I have converted from metric to US measurements, but exact quantities for some ingredients (such as spices) were not given; in such instances I have used my own judgement and intuition (as with the reserved shallots and pancetta). What follows is simply the method, devoid of story and Marlena's inimitable flair for language and style. (Humble apologies, Chou.)*

9-day Duck à la Marlena

Serves 2–4

Ingredients:

4 duck breasts, rinsed, dried, and layer of fat scored in hatch-mark pattern
bunch of fresh thyme
1½ tablespoon (25g) coarse sea salt (minimum; you may need more for 4 breasts)
25 white peppercorns, ground
25 allspice berries, crushed

—

½ dozen shallots, diced (I confess to using a dozen, an error in my notes, to good
   effect)
3.5 oz (100g) thick slice pancetta, coarsely diced
½ bottle (2 cups/475ml) Sauvignon Blanc or dry white wine

—

3 cups (700ml) "good red wine" (ample room for personal preference here)
1½ tablespoon unsalted butter, room temperature
2 teaspoons all-purpose flour
1 tablespoon dark brown sugar
¼ cup (60g) red currant preserves (often difficult to find in the States; opt for a
   red fruit blend or sour cherry)
4 cloves, crushed to a paste
2 teaspoons genuine balsamic vinegar (*aceto balsamico*)

—

½ cup dry Marsala
1 teaspoon fresh parsley, finely chopped

Method:
Day 1

After scoring the fat (careful to not cut into the flesh underneath), leaving the
main layer intact, trim any loose bits of fat from the duck breasts and reserve for
later (a week from now) in a small dish, covered (mine went "off" but you can
freeze it to prevent rancidity, then thaw when ready to proceed). Place the breasts
in a casserole or baking dish.

Grind the white pepper and allspice, mixing them together in a small dish. Strip the thyme leaves from the branches and then chop them. Sprinkle 1½ tablespoon coarse sea salt over the thyme, and then rub the herbed salt into the scored fat; flip and do the same with the unscored flesh. Sprinkle the allspice and white pepper over the breasts and massage it in. Cover the surface entirely with spices and salt. Enclose tightly in cling film/plastic wrap and set in the fridge for a week. Each day, massage a bit more thyme and a pinch of the allspice-pepper mix into the breasts.

Day 7

Melt the reserved fat with a spoonful of water over low heat; slowly, without stirring, allowing any crisp bits to form and fall to the bottom of the pan. Set aside.

Chop the shallots and cut the thick slices of pancetta into a coarse dice. In a large sauté pan, combine the rendered fat, crisp bits, shallots, and pancetta, and cook on low heat until the shallots are translucent and pancetta is well coloured. Transfer to a deep baking dish (earthenware or terracotta, preferably) with a lid.

In the sauté pan, in the film of fat that remains, over medium-high heat sear the duck breasts, fat down, until mahogany in colour, about 5 minutes. Turn and repeat on the flesh side. Transfer to the casserole with the aromatics.

Add one-third bottle of the white wine to the casserole; it should be enough to just float the breasts. Cover directly with parchment or baking paper, then a tight fitting lid. Place over a medium flame until the wine begins to simmer, then place in a 350°F/180°C oven.

At 45-minute intervals, dose with additional wine (¼ cup or less), each time turning the breasts. Give three dosings and turnings, for a total of two and a quarter-hour. Remove from the oven and allow to cool thoroughly, uncovered. When at room temperature, cover with cling film and lid, then refrigerate 4-6 hours or overnight.

Day 8

Scrape away the yellow fat that has congealed (reserve it for later) and transfer the breasts to a bowl. Place the casserole over a low flame to warm the juices. Using a slotted spoon, remove the bits of shallot and pancetta, reserving them for the final dish. Add any remaining white wine along with 2 cups of red; bring to a boil and reduce by one-third.

While the sauce reduces, work the softened butter into the flour in the palm of your hand until it forms a congealed, smooth mass (*beurre manie*), and then set aside.

Add another cup of red wine and reduce again by a quarter. Add the sugar, preserves, and cloves, and stir. Taste and add salt, if needed. With the sauce at a low simmer, add bits of *beurre manie*, stirring constantly to incorporate. The sauce should begin to thicken slightly and become glossy. Off the flame, add the *balsamico* and stir. Add the breasts back to the warm sauce; cover and refrigerate for a day.

Day 9

Preheat the oven to 300°F/150°C. Add ½ cup of dry Marsala to the pot and stir, then heat in a gentle oven for about an hour. Remove from the heat and let rest half a day.

When ready to serve, warm the reserved shallots and pancetta in a small pan, and add a small bit of chopped parsley. Add the remaining half-cup of red wine to the casserole and reheat to warm the duck and sauce.

Place the duck breasts in wide, shallow bowls. Top them with the warmed shallot and pancetta, spoon the sauce around, and finish with a pinch of parsley.

Savour unhurriedly with a contented sense of gratitude for the grace of the table and uncountable blessings of life.

❧ ❧ ❧

The Hummingbird of Devotion

(February, 2016)

This morning I lay in bed as my blurry eyes contemplated the soft, silver light illuminating heavy flaxen draperies, and with an inhale I gave my cells a positive word of thanks. Silently, I blessed myself.

I welcome good things and possibility today. I embrace mysterious grace, for I am never separate from the song of the world. I will leave the door of my heart ajar to catch sunlight and a soft wind from the sea that whispers through the garden.

Rising, I pulled on some clothes, nudged the thermostat up to make the noisy old furnace roar into action, and in the kitchen set the cobalt blue kettle atop a flame on the stove. In the living room, I drew back the leaf-stenciled linen curtains, switched off the front porch light, and then stepped barefoot in my usual way out to greet the morning. Three antique bronze bells jingled on their braided cord as I softly opened the front door, but the Sussex Duo were content in their bed under a blanket, not inclined to get up yet. And I left the door ajar behind me ... just as I said to my heart that I would.

The early morning air smelled sweetly of honey, perfumed by an abundance of flowering trees in the neighborhood, and the voice of the sea, usually a faint and crackling static, rumbled like distant thunder. I crossed the cool wooden deck to the old bricks, and then stepped onto the dirt where, laying my hands upon the Grandmother Monterey cypress, I opened my body in a gentle morning stretch.

So much in life seems fleeting like the delicate spring blossoms, yet this great venerable being, whose roughly furrowed trunk spirals gracefully like a corkscrew, reminds me of the enduring grace of nature. Wordlessly, she teaches patience and strength, the value of deep roots, as well as the generosity of offering shelter, and listening to stories without interruption or needing to reply. Blessed be, Grandmother, long may you stand.

I turned back towards the cottage, the eastern sky aglow as a bright ribbon above the roofline and stitched with tall silhouettes of neighbors' pine trees beyond. Inhaling, exhaling, breathing down into my bare soles, I opened my arms wide and sent a prayer towards the sunrise.

There are tasks to be accomplished today. Plenty of them. Some of what awaits is work I don't want to do but such is life. Maybe, just possibly, I can make a small shift in my attitude—like turning toward the rising sun—and face the day with less resistance, burden, and overwhelm.

Be soft and open, River.

Stepping back into the warmth of the house, I paused briefly on the threshold, my peripheral vision caught by the new acquisition outside the cottage windows: a hummingbird feeder.

After wanting one for the past year and a half of being here in California, yesterday I finally found just what I was wishing for. Most of the feeders I've encountered are cheap plastic things that lack beauty, craftsmanship, and allure (unless you're a hummingbird, I suppose). This one is made of red glass ("hummers" are drawn to red), and fashioned like an old-style bottle. It was not expensive, suited my budget, and has a very nice look that pleases me.

"Have nothing in your house that you do not know to be useful, or believe to be beautiful," said William Morris, the textile designer who strongly influenced the British Arts and Crafts Movement in the late 19th-century. His words are a motto I have taken deeply to heart, and when I came across the red glass feeder, a frisson of joy rippled through my core.

Back at home, I hung it on a bronze chain from the roof eaves outside the front windows. The table on the other side of the glass is usually where I sit to write (or edit) for long stretches of time if the day is not warm enough to be outdoors, and also where we eat our meals. A hummingbird feeder suspended where it can be seen at all hours seems simply perfect.

Curiously, perched on the interior white painted windowsill, sits a small, Japanese wooden sculpture of a hummingbird. The wings are outstretched as the bird hovers poised above two juveniles with open beaks in a nest, the adult's long slender beak the balancing point that holds the body aloft. A delicate and exquisite piece, it belonged to my adoptive mother and remains one of my most cherished treasures, something that I appreciate and admire every day. [Read "Hummingbirds and Communion," SAJ 2014, a post about poetry, nature, and grace.]

How I adore these miraculous little winged creatures of beauty. Some of them migrate south from California, but the Anna's hummingbird remains year round, and I often see—hear!—them zooming about when I am on a walk, especially in warmer weather. Yet with the perpetual shade of the Grandmother Monterey cypress, and a lack of alluring flowers at the front of the cottage, the hummers are not often around this residence. With the feeder, I am hoping to draw those flying jewels of inspiration and joy, so that I can sit by the window or on the deck and watch them hovering close at hand—ones made of vivid feathers and rapid breath rather than carved wood.

Sometimes the path at one's feet feels like a rocky one, an uphill climb, or both. Often one's work seems to have little immediate or tangible benefit; we struggle and toil day after day, climbing some mountain, yet the trail just goes on out of sight around the next bend. And while beauty and inspiration are everywhere—even in ravaged places, and if only in the expression of human kindness—if we aren't paying attention or the heart is shuttered, we may fail to recognize or heed what calls softly to us. In previous posts, I have mused on ways that we might welcome and invite *grace*; hanging the red glass hummingbird feeder outside my front windows is a quietly symbolic act for just that—invoking a colored flash of grace and wild beauty.

Beyond my occupation of healing work with clients, I've been wrestling with the ongoing task of building an author's "platform" as L.R. Heartsong. Grappling alternately with expectation and disappointment, I found myself reflecting, *what is devotion?*

No small thought, this, for surely *devotion* fathoms the depths of faith, love, work, creativity, and soul. Already it is clear I need to sit and also walk in contemplation—meditating on the contours and complexities of its deeper meaning. However, even in initial moments of reflection, along with qualities such as *dedication* and *willingness*, undoubtedly a key part it involves *giving*—even when such an act seems difficult or challenging. Perhaps especially then. We are prone to take endlessly, ever grasping and wanting, but what do we give in return or exchange?

As with *The Bones and Breath*, this weekly journal column is part of my offering: a small way of giving something back to the 'more-than-human' world. The Earth sustains us all, whether we recognize it consciously or not, and I endeavor to live with an ongoing song-chant-prayer of gratitude. And *hope*. Some days I fare better than others. Yet week in, week out, what I do in these posts is offer a hymn—to you, Nature, the Wild Beloved, and the Larger Story that I simply call *the Mystery*. And in doing so, it opens the door of my own heart.

At times, life seems more like work than a celebration. When it feels that way, I know it is up to me to adjust the focus and reframe my experience, whether through gratitude or seeking inspiration as a Soul Artist. Somehow I must realign with *willingness* rather than resistance, and then circle back to *giving*—as if it were the heartbeat of devotion to something larger than myself, which of course it is.

I recall some years ago a friend in Santa Fe, New Mexico, relayed an interview she had just listened to (or possibly read) with an elderly, local artist who was still actively creating and producing art. When asked about the secret of her longevity, success, and continued output, her answer was that every day she actively sought out three things to inspire her. Brilliant.

Just as the Grandmother Monterey cypress gently teaches and reminds me about life, when I gaze at the exquisite sculpture of the hummingbird feeding its young, I am shown something about devotion. One embodiment of it, at least.

Perhaps soon a zooming, live hummingbird will appear and hover at the red glass feeder by the front window for the first time, delighting and inspiring me. In the meantime, I will continue to find modest ways each day of welcoming nature, magic, and grace—mostly by being rooted in the moment(s) through my senses, and appreciating the beauty and *feel* of things.

Friend, as I so often encourage here, walk barefoot on the earth. Consider *sacred reciprocity*—whatever that might mean to you—as a practice, offering something of beauty in exchange for the sensual gift of being ensouled in a human body. Water the garden and pull weeds. Create a nice, fresh meal for your beloved or a friend. Unapologetically hug a tree. Thank a farmer. Feed the birds. Sing, if only just to lift your own heart.

Find, and somehow show, your devotion to something bigger than work or yourself.

Most importantly, no matter the weather, leave the door of the heart ajar.

❧ ❧ ❧

Where the Elk Dream

(October, 2016)

Give me mountains, please. *These mountains*, I smile, as I drive up into the western front of the crumpled, arid range that always feels like home.

From the high desert plateau at seven thousand feet, the squat piñon and dwarf junipers slowly yield to tall Ponderosa pines and shimmering aspens crowding the higher elevations. At a familiar spot, overlooking the endless painted horizon of New Mexico's vastness, I park my car at a trailhead where I step onto the day's path, anticipation buzzing lightly in my core.

Generally, I walk my chosen trail for a bit, allowing lungs to accustom to the thin, crisp air as I steadily leave the car and road behind. A small backpack, wide-brimmed ivory canvas hat, water flask, a bag of raw almonds, fountain pen and journal; along with my soft-shell windbreaker, this is all that I carry. Senses open wide, I reach out to touch, welcome, and praise the sensuous beauty that enfolds.

At some indeterminate point, two things happen. First, my shoes come off, stashed in the pack, and I move on barefoot. Exposed sole and soul communing with soil. And then, guided by an invisible compass—a glimmer of sunlight through the trees, the swift flash of a bird's wing, the curious temptation of a rock formation away from the trail, or just whispering intuition—heeding my allurement, I invariably leave the primary track behind. Often my bare feet follow narrow game paths left by deer or elk, wondering where the elusive four-leggeds go in the bright light of the dayworld.

Accustomed to living at high altitude, my body feels light and open, and though I am a two-legged stranger in this wild milieu, through regular visits and paying attention via my senses, it feels that I belong here if only in some modest way. Moving along the trail, relishing nature undisturbed and non-domesticated, a soft hum of recognition echoes in my own bones—the ancient, genetic part of me that still belongs to *wilderness*.

Such goodness, this clear autumn day in October high in the Sangre de Cristo mountains above Santa Fe, where once again I've abandoned the leaf-littered path to follow a whisper of an animal trail along the western slope. From the signs— broken branches, rubbed tree limbs, large hoof prints, newly flattened grass and fresh droppings—elk have recently passed this way, perhaps last night or early in the morning's light.

Climbing a rise on the mountain's ancient shoulder, I emerge from resin-scented pines into a spacious grove of towering silver-white aspen, their autumnal crowns of fluttering gold leaves shining brightly against the turquoise sky. Native, knee-high grasses are pale and dried as old straw, and treading the trampled non-trail I note throughout the glade that the lanky stalks have been flattened into large, oblong ovals. Here, as a small herd, the elk bedded down.

I halt in my tracks, gazing at the grassy indentations while the wind whispers endlessly overhead, a jingling of ten thousand paper-thin golden coins as aspen leaves.

I know where the elk dream.

Slipping the daypack from my shoulders, I walk tenderly through the glen, feeling the earth and dried grasses underfoot, looking for a place to sit and write. Drawn by the elk beds, I step gingerly into one of the mammal-leveled spaces in-between two trees. Then I prop my rucksack against the smooth, dusty white bark of the nearest aspen and sit down, running my hands delicately over the compacted vegetation as if feeling a fine carpet. Sunlight warms my shoulders and suddenly my eyelids feel heavy, a sense of gentle gravity weighting my limbs, lulling me toward a nap.

Like a child curling up on his mother's empty bed, I lie down on my side with knees drawn toward my chest in fetal position. Folding my hiking jacket as a pillow, there amid the murmurs of a cool breeze in the golden boughs overhead, feeling held in the welcoming arms of Grandmother Earth, I slip into autumn dreams.

When my eyes reopen sometime later, the afternoon light, white fluffy clouds, and shadows in the grove have shifted, yet the aspens are still singing softly, a chorus in the endless song of the world. Sitting upright, I prop myself against the tree trunk, and with pen and notebook in hand allow my gaze to wander though the surroundings, easy tides of breath rolling soft and full in my belly.

I wonder, what is here to be discovered? What part of Creation wishes to be seen and admired, marveled over and wondered upon...?

Possibly I'll spy a creature moving about, or some ordinary treasure resting at my feet, like the remnants of a paper wasps' nest I found last week that had been torn apart by a windstorm. A discarded antler or a jawbone crusted with dirt. Smaller, there is simply the incomprehensibly complex relationship of life entwined in even an inch of dry soil and fallen leaves under my fingers. And I know it is always a shift in perspective that allows us to finally see what appears.

Dreaming in an elk bed ...

These forays of mine into wild places, where so often I leave the path behind, always reveal more than merely *tracking*. My solitary wanderings are really about *seeing*. Listening. Remembering. *Feeling*. Waking up to all my senses and the uncivilized soul—that oft-forgotten counterbalance to my well-domesticated being. The rugged, barefoot bohemian wearing bear claws and chunks of turquoise versus the groomed sybarite and aesthete with a Mont Blanc fountain pen.

Welcoming the whole of myself within the *greater* self and soul that is Nature.

No matter where we reside, the mundane details of life tend to dull us into a sort of stupor: daily work, patterns in relationships, errands, and an endless parade of distractions. Little exists to remind us of the Larger Story unfolding, and we have mostly lost and forgotten the sacred. Even if one has created a home that feels like a sanctuary, full of precious objects that speak to the soul, amid routine the familiar becomes commonplace. Unseen. Whether it is a lovely altar adorned with beeswax candles, a fabulous piece of art, or the most stunning display of nature's beauty beyond our windows, we quickly habituate to it.

I walk in wild places not simply to exercise but to wake up and rediscover my deepest, most authentic self. Roaming in nature, I slip away from the usual and open to the extraordinary once more, seduced by mystery and untamed beauty, falling in love again and again with the humblest of things... with life itself.

Somewhere along a narrow trail or beneath the outstretched arms of a noble tree, beside a laughing creek or in the acrid-smelling hole of a fox den, my most authentic soul waits for me to come and find it today.

I know this, *everything is alive*. Everything speaks. And the world is full of wild magic for those who can see, listen, and truly feel. And I know too that I belong to that mystical realm with each and every passing breath.

Earth is *dreaming us* awake—through all manner of means and messages—but among the uncountable multitudes only a few of us are listening. Today, as autumn descends in painted glory, welcoming the season of bountiful harvest and slow letting go, I am listening for that guidance. Turning toward my allurement. Trusting a strange resonance in bones and breath, becoming a singular, harmonic note in the song of the world.

And I know where the elk dream.

❧ ❧ ❧

[This post was adapted from one of my personal journal entries in 2008 when I resided in northern New Mexico.]

Tea Leaves and Transitions: Finding Grace
(December, 2016)

Seated upon an upholstered chair near the fireplace, cradling an ivory porcelain cup in my hands, I stare into its depths and contemplate the patterns of broken tea leaves.

I'm deeply fond of this Asian-style vessel; simple and unadorned, round without a handle, with a ceramic infuser resting inside and removed when the brew has steeped. Actually, I own two such cups, nearly identical; one is celadon green, and this creamy white one that looks as if it were fashioned of glossy bone. Both are finished with a *crackle glaze* that, over time, tea has stained to the effect of fine brown spiderwebs within the cup and infuser. Despite the very small holes of the insert, little fragments of leaves manage to slip through and sink to the bottom, where they twirl and dance as I drink, briefly settling into abstract patterns before they shift again. And again.

In the quiet of a December afternoon with a cold grey sky beyond the windows, two English Whippets asleep for their fourth nap of the day and my partner elsewhere with his mum, in the tranquility of the cottage my gaze is drawn by the leaf bits in the depths of this dear cup. Contemplating them as if I might somehow augur the future from their seemingly random arrangement, at first I see a hare leaping over the moon. Then a griffin embracing Europe. With each sip and swirl, the vision changes.

The past weeks have been a time of change, both within and without, as gilded leaves fall from the trees, the very heralds of transition. It feels like a chapter of life is soon ending and a new one beginning, and while I perceive the door swinging closed I do not yet see one opening. Moments come upon me when I feel a bit lost or stuck, as if the silver fog has rolled in again and the track I've been following is suddenly obscured or vanished, with only the ghostly silhouettes of windswept Monterey cypress trees as silent sentinels.

My partner is preparing to leave his director's job (which is based elsewhere) in the coming months, and it is unlikely we will remain in this quaint little town by the sea. The time is soon coming to move once again. Self-employed for years, my work—healing arts, soul-based coaching, and writing—is more or less transportable, and I am no stranger to being repotted and transplanted. Yet it feels like an evolution in my occupation is at hand, particularly as I deepen into an apprenticeship with sacred plant medicines—launched during my mysterious illness, electromagnetic hypersensitivity (EHS), and general unraveling last spring. A shamanic initiation is underway for this reluctant mystic.

At odd moments in all this, whether washing the dishes or walking the Sussex Duo, I have found myself musing on the nature of *transition*. Do we always recognize beginnings as they unfurl? Or endings, for that matter? Might we lean into the challenges and changes to welcome them, rather than attempting to hold fast or push them away, wishing for something different? Easier said than done, no doubt.

I sense and hear new ventures calling like voices on the wind, just ahead yet out of sight, and feel a readiness—an urgency, almost—to move on to meet them. Tangled in this is my ongoing longing to finally stop roaming, to settle on some patch of earth with tall trees, and sink roots into dark, rich soil (and soul); knowing that my next work, or the emergent expression of my current offerings, can *only* grow from that place—much like C.G. Jung and his stone tower at Bollingen, or O'Keeffe in her adobe house on the mesa at Abiquiu. Such knowing has haunted me since May, and even earlier, but now the prescience feels nearly overbearing. [Read "Roots for the Soul," May 2016] My partner, too, is ready for the change and though both of us are weary of life in our proverbial, painted gypsy caravan, ever rolling on to some new campsite, we share the sense of hovering at a threshold. And the new thing, unformed and still mysterious, will finally arrive *only when we let go*.

Even for travelers and nomads, transitions are not always easy. To simply be in a place of uncertainty, to trust that a portal of opportunity will open or the bridge appear, requires its own measure of psychological maturity and faith. Even when the sacred spark of intention seeds the quantum Field of Possibility, still a period of gestation and growth ensues—the time needed for manifestation. A *sacred waiting,* that irrespective of focused intent cannot be hurried or rushed. Things arrive or ripen like sweet fruit on their own schedule, not ours. And I've learned—am *still* learning— that curious blessings exist in this, too.

During the past month, moments of uncertainty have found me outside, drawing the cool coastal air deep into my lungs, bare feet on the earth for daily Qigong, or simply laying hands upon the rough grey bark of the Grandmother Monterey cypress. Gently coaxing myself to open the tight places of constriction still held by rusted, iron fingers of doubt.

Be here. Now. All weather passes eventually. You are ever guided and cared for, and it isn't possible to fail.

Here. Now. My eyes sweep the familiar space of our front room recently decorated for the winter holidays, with stockings hung upon the brick fireplace. I breathe more deeply into chest and belly, attempting to see it as *festive* rather than simply cluttered, reminding myself that it's only for a few weeks of the year. George Winston's classic piano album "December" plays softly in the background, the cottage smells invitingly of spices and citrus, the old furnace rumbles loudly as a military tank, and beyond the windows the great trunk of the Grandmother is streaked darkly with rain.

With a last sip of fragrant Jasmine White Monkey, my gaze returns to the dark green bits at the bottom, considering them once more, as if through their arrangement I might decipher the way forward—or at least the shape and nature of this current transition. I swirl the nearly empty cup a final time, recasting the fragments and deliberating their placement, looking to change my own fate and future with such a facile gesture. Yet I know the only real movement needing to be made is an ongoing, humble opening of the heart, saying *yes* to the path ahead wherever it may lead and whatever it brings.

Surrender. Trust. Let go.

Autumn draws to its close, the painted time of harvesting, while the slow turning inward continues—spiraling us deeper into shorter days and lengthening darkness. I am searching for the blessings in this, too. All things turn and pass away, and I know there isn't any point holding on as the wheel revolves. One's palm must be open for a gift to be placed within it, which cannot happen if we are clinging to something already. Anything. Too, I remind myself that the path is simply to *appreciate beauty every day*; if we cannot find it where we are, then to go in search of it, while striving to create something of beauty ourselves, offering it selflessly and shamelessly forward.

Here, beside the flashing sea, the moment feels fraught with uncertainty—like a leaf still welded to bare branch, wondering when the conspiracy of wind and gravity will help it detach, to then spiral down and land gently upon the patient earth. Yet there are too many blessings each day to count.

Holding the empty cup with its final fanning of fragments, inexplicably words from Rumi flash through my mind, lines of a poem I recently encountered that struck my heart:

"I know you are tired, but come. This is the way."

Gentle reader, the road goes on and on, disappearing around the bend. Here's hoping you will find the gifts in your challenges and the grace of transitions, while welcoming the simple, ordinary minutes of the day. Turn off the so-called news; it fills the world with angst and bitterness. Instead, as I have so often encouraged in this Journal over the years, create little rituals that anchor you in the beauty of the moment and *nourish* somehow—like a tranquil cup of tea, or a deep breath where your heart opens and blooms once again to the myriad blessings that surround. No matter the path you are walking or trailblazing on your own, each of us can be an offering of goodness to the 'more-than-human' world.

Frequently, I remind myself that the entire Universe has conspired to bring about this wrinkle of spacetime. Thus undoubtedly, everything is *precisely* where it needs to be—challenges, uncertainty, and all—even though the reasons remain unclear from the current vantage point.

Spiraling onward, we go, welcoming the season's blessings and leaning into mysterious grace.

Always grace, I say.

☙ ☙ ☙

Come Darkness, Come Light

(December, 2016)

In predawn shadows I am awake, snuggled beside my mate in the warm cocoon of a goose down duvet, hearing the small, insistent voice telling me to go outdoors to greet the dawn—or the darkness, on this longest night of the year.

Rising from bed and pulling on clothes, I move through a familiar routine: nudging up the manual thermostat in the hallway and making my way to the darkened kitchen where, without turning on a light, I place the cobalt blue kettle atop a hissing flame to boil. In the front room, I switch on the tiny lights of our miniature Charlie Brown Christmas tree, and then strike a match and hold it to the wicks of two candles on the table nearby. In the soft glow, I pull back the sheer linen draperies—fabric too thin to offer suitable insulation against the winter outside—feeling the chill through old glass as I peer through the panes into December darkness.

Donning the navy blue cardigan I generally wear around the house, and picking up an heirloom black pottery bowl from the Santa Clara Pueblo in New Mexico, I open the front door and step out into the cold air. For a moment, I stand with the carved vessel held against my heart, offering silent thanks to the powers that be, then gently set down the Blessing Bowl in front of the praying frog sculpture from Bali. The wooden boards of the deck feel frozen beneath my bare soles, icily jolting me fully awake, yet I linger silently for a minute, observing the faint pattern of moonshadows cast by the protective arms of the Grandmother Monterey cypress, a lacy pattern of silver and charcoal in a blanket thrown down.

Springing my senses wide to the shadows, I welcome whatever comes. Gathering the low voice of the sea in the distance, and a resinous, almost lemony fragrance of New World cypresses, the passing rumble of a few early cars along the main road a few streets away, the bright dawn stars twinkling in a clear sky. The imposing presence of the venerable tree that watches over this artist's cottage. All amid the relative hush of the surrounding world before it wakes to noise, activity, and busyness.

Crossing the deck, my breath forms frosty clouds in the air. The even colder bricks underfoot deliver a further shock as I approach the Grandmother, so I step gratefully onto soil less frozen than the masonry, and lay hands upon the roughened grey bark of her great, spiraling trunk.

Breathing in, breathing out.

The entirety of the modest front garden rests in shadows and night guise. Facing east, I raise my arms to the familiar lineup of trees silhouetted against a pale blue ribbon of light stretched across the sky. A promise of the coming dawn. From here, outside looking in, the miniature lights of our little faux tree and the candles flickering offer a welcome, cheery glow—beckoning me back inside to warmth and a cup of good tea.

Silently, I offer my litany of gratitude, giving thanks for the blessings of the day *and those already on their way*—earthy connection underfoot a tactile reminder of the Larger Story enfolding us all. Nimbly, I step back across the cold deck and, with a final inhale of darkness and coastal air, cross the threshold into warm, human realms.

My mate and our English Whippets, the Sussex Duo, remain tucked into respective beds, loathe to rise from deep winter dreaming, but I am up in typical fashion to greet the holy and spend some solitary time in quiet, expanded awareness. Something not quite *meditation*, at least not any sort of formal technique. Today is December 21st, the winter solstice, and it seems especially relevant to offer thanks on a day when a new season officially comes on stage, the previous one bowing out.

In years previous, I have written SAJ posts about the solstice; how it became my chosen winter holiday, along with the tradition of a feast with friends or family gathered around our festive table—welcoming the essential gifts of *darkness*, as well as those of *light*. In these past weeks and months, given the turbulent political climate and global events, I've penned more than a few words about the hidden worth of shadows and the transforming nature of our challenges, always interwoven with blessings if we can discern the golden threads.

On this shortest day of the year, winter arrives fully upon us; a dark chrysalis spun equally of mystery, constellations, and strange grace. The time of in-gathering and harvest has passed, just like the painted leaves fallen from trees, and now as dormant seeds in a dreaming time we wait… imagining what we may become.

Seated in the high-backed French armchair that each morning I rotate to face my altar, with chilled hands wrapped around a steaming cup of tea and feet enrobed in thick wool socks, I find myself nostalgic for winter solstices of years past. Missing the *bonhomie* around our well-traveled table while feasting with those who are dear to us. Instead, with little community here or roots, ever the wanderers, my partner and I are navigating another passage of transition. Once again we are letting go of roles, work, and attachments—just like those failing leaves—yet still tending a few precious dreams wrapped in the silk of prayers. All the while quietly waiting for guidance and opportunity to move us forward into the next chapter of life; unclear where our painted gypsy caravan will roll toward next, knowing only it will carry us away from this dear little seaside town amid the trees and swirling mists.

Whither now, I wonder. Each day holding the Blessing Bowl outstretched, gathering life into my heart with gratitude.

Later this morning, we will stroll our favourite oceanside path just south of town, perhaps with the Sussex Duo or not, and perch upon a familiar wooden bench while churning blue waves serenade and hypnotize us, watching California sea otters cavort and float in the surf, grateful for a winter day fair enough to allow such an outing. To uplift the soul and inspire, little is better than a dose of wild nature and a far line of horizon—widening perspective and inviting us into possibility once more.

The noisy, rattling furnace finally shuts off, flooding my belly with relief; for a few minutes, the cottage lapses back into sweet silence. This 1940's residence is poorly insulated and thin, single-pane windows cause it to hemorrhage heat quickly. Soon, the old and inefficient heater, loud as a military tank, will rumble on again, but in the early morning quietude I savour the intervals of blissful silence.

Breathing in, breathing out... *holy, holy.*

Given that our tribe is far flung elsewhere, as nomads we celebrate these year-end holidays in a low-key fashion. Long ago we bowed out of the typical gift exchange obligations (other than with each other), thus pleasantly removed from the chaos and crass materialism that Christmas has largely become. Aided even more by the fact we don't watch or even own a television, the holidays feel pleasantly non-commercial and non-pressured. With very deliberate *simpleness,* somehow the winter holiday season is both homey *and* elegant—really, what could be better than that? At any moment of the day, repeatedly I find myself awash in gratitude for all the unassuming treasures of life, and always there are too many to count, scattered and disguised amongst the seeming challenges. The ordinary sacred, yes, indeed.

Tonight's solstice dinner will just be three of us, and so too at Christmas four days hence. After a half day of cooking and preparations as I putter in the kitchen, we will dine on a fresh spinach salad with dried cranberries, toasted pumpkin seeds, and best-quality crumbled Stilton, followed by little mushroom hand pies and a bubbling gratin of butternut squash and red onions. I have been dreaming of a dark gingerbread cake—fragrant, spicy, moist, and dense—with sliced pears fanned on top, and soon I will set about baking that; anticipation heightened further by the thought of it as a perfect accompaniment for tea in the days ahead. And there are chestnuts to roast, albeit in a cast iron pan rather than on an open fire, so I can have slightly sweet, warm nibbles to eat out of hand (whisking me back to dear France).

The dark reaches its zenith tonight—or perhaps its nadir—the longest night of the year, and the day's light slowly increases once more. I have spent the past decade celebrating *darkness* as a soulful mystery, opting not to push it away or just wishing it to end, but appreciating the unique gifts, challenges, dreaming-magic and power of it. This year, in our latest passage of transition, doing our best to lean into and embrace uncertainty, it feels especially right to welcome the *light* returning.

In a recent post, I shared that I sense the coming changes on the sea air and feel it in my bones. Yet it seems more like the dawn approaching after a long, dark night—perhaps as if we are emerging from a troubled, disturbing dream. Once again, the Gregorian calendar year draws to its close and we spiral on, dancing with riddles of fate and destinies we have chosen. Another jubilee of endings and new beginnings, hopeful as those may be. And as celebrations fade, summoning *willingness* and *patience* in one's heart, especially when the road seems difficult, long, and uphill.

In my ongoing soulful enquiry and healing journey, I've been musing on what is asked of us by *life itself*. A few weeks ago, seated in a morning meditation, I was suddenly enfolded by the strong perfume of lilies, as if an angel was near. (In the spirit of confession, angelic visits have been a repeated experience for this reluctant mystic over the years.) In my mind's eye and some *other* sense that escapes easy definition, I felt and heard the Archangel Raphael, the Healer, saying, "Each day, shine your light into the world."

His message filled me with warmth rippling like waves, a sense of wonder, and deep humility. And my sense was not that he was instructing me personally, as if I were someone special or chosen, so much as it was an invitation for *all* of us; that we might spend even a few minutes *consciously* sending luminescence into the shadow that engulfs much of the planet right now in humanity's evolutionary process.

Surely this is what is asked in return for the gift of being alive: some sort of *sacred reciprocity*. Breathing in and out, a soul full of gratitude for the darkly tangled beauty of it all, whilst striving to offer a measure of beauty and goodness in exchange.

The light returns, my friend. And a candle loses nothing by lighting another candle.

As this round of winter holidays enfolds us, whether you celebrate the solstice or Yule, the Christ's birthday, Hanukkah, or something else entirely, here's hoping that your heart is unlocked and welcoming. Not simply for gifts of grace and illumination, but for the challenges and curious treasures of darkness, too. Truly, only in the shadows do we find our own light.

Through these holidays and beyond, as we voyage through the cosmos on this blue-green jewel of a planet, may you celebrate the precious gift of being alive on a mysterious, beautiful, and sometimes difficult journey.

Breathing in, breathing out.

Come darkness, come light, we will dwell in possibility.

❧ ❧ ❧

Acknowledgments

Throughout the Soul Artist Journal years, my trusty Paris fountain pen in hand (every post was hand-written), from both nature and people I routinely drew inspiration, perspective, strength, and willingness to continue with the weekly *giveaway*. A few of those sources deserved special mention, which I have done in the previous two volumes of this SAJ trilogy.

❧

Since closing the cover on the Journal and moving on to other ventures, I have been deeply grateful for those who found and followed my work (in all its various formats), especially the ones that reached out with words of sincere appreciation, and readers who shared the offerings with others. Bless you.

Apart from my role as a writer/author, for three decades it has been my great privilege to work with a diverse array of clients seeking healing and transformation, individuals as well as groups. From my own healing journey and personal evolution, I know how very difficult it is to clear the entrenched patterns and past wounding, to forgive others and self, and find an authentic soul path in service to something larger. Collectively, you have softened and widened this man's heart, mirrored to me the power of vulnerability, and forged my deep compassion for our innate humanness. As I say every day, *bless us all.*

Boundless appreciation for graphic designer, Katie Boyer Clark, who teamed with me on all three retrospectives in the SAJ series. Your keen eye, along with a penchant for uncluttered design and appealing aesthetic, has been invaluable in creating these little feasts of soulful nourishment. It's a delight to work with you, dear, a thousand thank you's and more.

❧

Now, onwards we go, spiraling deeper into the unfathomable Mystery with just one true imperative: *evolve.* May we each do so with whatever grace can be summoned, a heart open to the beauty, and an intent to create goodness in the world.

❧ ❧ ❧

About the Author

L.R. Heartsong is a healer who writes, teaching a sensual connection with life, nature, and the soul of the world.

A body-centered therapist trained in somatic psychology, he became a Paris-trained chef (briefly a cook for the rich and famous), until his intuition and heart led him back to the healing arts, along with nature-based soul work.

Living in England, a revelation while crossing a Kentish field at twilight propelled him to write *The Bones & Breath: A Man's Guide to Eros, the Sacred Masculine, and the Wild Soul.* Upon returning to America, as part of his quest to get the book published, he launched the *Soul Artist Journal,* which slowly grew in popularity.

After nearly five years of weekly posts (2012–2017), Heartsong closed the cover on the Journal and began *TendingSacred*: lengthier, monthly writing along a healer's path (2017–2019). He has been a featured presenter on multiple podcasts as well as global online symposiums featuring change-making influencers (scientists, shamans, mystics, psychologists, healers, and more).

His first book won a Nautilus Book Award for Personal Growth & Self-Help.

LRHeartsong.com